DISCARDED

LEISURE IN THE MODERN WORLD

NRPA Recreation and Park Perspective Collection

edited by Dr. Diana R. Dunn
Director of Research
National Recreation and Park Association

Education through Play	Curtis, H.	$19.00
Education through Recreation	Jacks, L.	$13.00
Education by Plays and Games	Johnson, G.	$15.00
The New Leisure Challenges for the Schools	Lies, E.	$17.00
Play in Education	Lee, J.	$25.00
Play and Mental Health	Davis, J.	$15.00
Education through Recreation	Johnson, G.	$10.00
The Practical Conduct of Play	Curtis, H.	$19.00
The Play Movement	Rainwater, C.	$21.00
The Play Movement and its Significance	Curtis, H.	$19.00
Playground Technique and Playcraft	Leland, A. & L.	$17.00
American Playgrounds	Mero, E.	$17.00
Leisure in the Modern World	Burns, C.	$15.00
The Threat of Leisure	Cutten, G.	$12.00
The Normal Course of Play	NRA	$16.00
The Education of the Whole Man	Jacks, L.	$12.00
The Challenge of Leisure	Pack, A.	$14.00
Off the Job Living	Romney, G.	$15.00
A Philosophy of Play	Gulick, L.	$16.00
Europe at Play	Weir, L.	$45.00
Music in American Life	Zanzig, A.	$28.00
Music in Institutions	Van de Wall, W.	$35.00
The First County Park System	Kelsey, F.	$15.00
County Parks	NRA	$14.00
Central Park—First Annual Report	New York	$14.00
The Spirit of Youth and the City Streets	Addams, J.	$12.00
Annals March 1910	AAP&SS	$16.00
Municipalization of Play and Recreation	Fulk, J.	$10.00
Luther Halsey Gulick	Dorgan, E.	$14.00
Constructive and Preventive Philanthropy	Lee, J.	$15.00

order from:

MC GRATH PUBLISHING COMPANY
821 Fifteenth Street N.W.
Washington, D.C.

LEISURE
IN THE
MODERN WORLD

BY
C. DELISLE BURNS

McGrath Publishing Company

&

NATIONAL RECREATION AND PARK ASSOCIATION

WASHINGTON, D.C.

COPYRIGHT, 1932, BY THE CENTURY CO.
ALL RIGHTS RESERVED, INCLUDING THE
RIGHT TO REPRODUCE THIS BOOK, OR
PORTIONS THEREOF, IN ANY FORM. 392

First Printing

LC#75-143049
ISBN 0-8434-0434-5

PRINTED IN U. S. A.

PREFACE

Leisure is a favorite subject with preachers; for all preachers know what other people ought to do. But this book is not a sermon. It is an attempt at analyzing certain new tendencies in the actual uses of leisure in what is here called the modern world. The modern world, for this purpose, means the complex of new customs and attitudes, which has arisen, out of the earlier industrialism, within the past half century. Older uses of leisure therefore are referred to here, only by way of contrast. But the analysis of facts is followed by a discussion of new social ideals; and the second part of the book deals with contemporary tendencies in "social movements" and current social standards.

The book is based upon a series of "Talks" which I gave on the Radio from Glasgow and London in 1932. I have retained the informality of radio speech but added some sections that would not so easily be followed on the radio. The argument of the book runs thus. Recent changes in the amount of leisure and in its uses have caused social tendencies toward experimentalism in daily life, toward equality and toward "movements" which aim at modifying the traditional position of women, of children, and of the youthful. There is now a possibility of a new type of civilized life, not dependent upon a leisured class but arising directly from the leisure of those who work for a living. This civilization would be "democratic" if that obscure word may be used to mark the contrast with all former civilizations—all of which have been based upon the assumptions of a "slave society."

The student of the social sciences will understand that this book is an essay in culture, not in political science nor in economics. But it may be worth noting that, from one point of view, it is a study of "consumption." Unfortunately the social sciences are still so completely dominated by economics that even the words "consumption" or "use" may be misinterpreted. The obsolete psychology which underlies the terminology of modern economics and of the traditional political science cannot be corrected here; but I do not assume that any of the authorities in these subjects are competent to provide the language adequate for the interpretation of modern life. Differences in "consumption," which is often confused with "distribution," and in "use" are qualitative and cannot be rendered statistically. But social sciences which omit to note the methods of cooking potatoes in their concentration upon the price of potatoes, are quite futile as bases for public policy. With such "economics" it is quite easy to prove that "we" cannot afford leisure or education: indeed it is doubtful whether "we" can afford to live!

I have added in an appendix a very few of the

letters which were written to me, while I gave the series of Talks, because they indicate the sort of evidence on which I have drawn, in my visits to many different social circles in Europe and America.

C. Delisle Burns

London, England
June 10, 1932

CONTENTS

CHAPTER   PAGE

I. THE INCREASE OF LEISURE 3

Recent increase in amount of leisure and in the number of ways of using it, due to certain economic and sociological changes. But the new leisure itself becomes a source of new changes in social customs and standards.

II. THE NEW FOOD AND CLOTHING 17

A higher level of common comfort in new foods and new clothing, as well as more similar customs, has promoted a tendency toward experimentalism in everyday life.

III. THE HOME IN THE MODERN WORLD . . . 36

As an instrument for living, the house and its furnishings are being changed to meet modern needs; and as a complex of human relationships the "home" is changing in the relation of husband and wife and in that of parent and child. But the change is not as great as it might be.

IV. THE SOCIAL EFFECTS OF MOTOR-CARS . . . 55

Motor-cars in common use extend the range of acquaintance with the world: they make manners more similar and, if they make some people superficial, on the whole their effect is good in uprooting the mind.

CONTENTS

CHAPTER   PAGE

V. MOVING PICTURES AND RADIO 75

The new machines for entertainment depend upon millions with small incomes. They produce by conscious policy in some countries, by accident in others, a similar outlook in great numbers. They increase the range of interests of the majority and diminish distinctions between social classes.

VI. WAYS OF ESCAPE 96

Leisure is used for escape from the commonplace. Two significant new uses of it for such a purpose are gambling and "hiking." Betting on sporting events aims at excitement or money gains. Hiking is a revolt against the city-area. In both the crust of acquiescence is broken.

VII. CONVENTIONS AND MODERNITY 115

Manners are changing in character. New conventions are being formed and old conventions given new meanings. In general the new manners are those of a community of equals, at ease in converse with strangers.

VIII. LEISURE AND THE WOMAN'S MOVEMENT . . 135

As soon as leisure is used by those who work, their attention to public affairs causes social movements. The Woman's Movement is typical. Some approach has been made toward equality of status for men and women in social intercourse, partly as an accidental result of new conditions, partly as the result of a "movement."

CONTENTS

CHAPTER   PAGE

IX. CHILDREN'S LEISURE 155

Children are fewer in the modern world and freer and healthier. Their leisure has been greatly affected by moving pictures and by new movements such as the Scout Movement. There is a tendency toward social equality among children even in Great Britain.

X. A REVOLT OF YOUTH 178

The "revolt of youth" is a normal phenomenon now occurring in a new world of machines and skepticism. The youth to-day is less frightened, more independent, and more determined to go its own way, even if genuine Youth Movements are "captured" by the old gangs in politics and religion.

XI. CIVILIZATION AND THE LEISURED CLASS . . . 201

The function of a leisured class in the traditional "slave" societies of the past can now be performed in the leisure of those who work. This may improve the quality and it will certainly change the character of the finest products of leisure.

XII. NEW LEISURE MAKES NEW MEN 219

The old ideals of the "gentleman" and the "lady" are being replaced by new ideals of character and community. The new type of man or woman has more vitality and less aloofness.

XIII. CAN DEMOCRACY BE CIVILIZED? 239

Social equality may not cause a higher level to be reached in the arts and sciences. Restlessness

CHAPTER		PAGE
	and superficiality may cause "externalism" of spirit; but there are signs of the "inner life" even under modern conditions.	
XIV.	PUBLIC POLICY	257
	The principles of current policy are obsolete. The new production has not yet affected men's minds. Saving is obsolete. Increase of leisure and education should be the major purposes of public policy.	
XV.	PRIVATE ENTERPRISE	272
	Enterprise in "consumption" or "use" has never been studied. But each man lives for himself, not merely for future ages: spontaneous enjoyment in leisure has no further purpose. It is final.	
	APPENDIX: Extracts from letters	289
	INDEX	301

LEISURE IN THE MODERN WORLD

I

THE INCREASE OF LEISURE

LEISURE is the most valuable product of modern mechanisms and modern social organization; but it is generally regarded as a negligible by-product and it is largely wasted. Spare time is still too often regarded as valueless. Public inquiries have been made into the waste of power and material in production. What were once regarded as useless by-products of one industry are now the bases for many other industries; and more wealth has been made by using what was wasted than was made from the original product. But leisure is still unconsidered.

Suppose, however, that one took spare time seriously. Suppose that we set our minds to discover the place of the by-product—spare time—in an industrial community which has devoted much energy to the increase of wealth and very little to a consideration of its uses. Suppose we saw what could be made of leisure. We should at any rate produce more of it; and perhaps we should be less incompetent in its distribution. The result might be a form of civilized life which would redeem the barbarism of the industrial system by abolishing the oppression of poverty and the futilities of private wealth.

Leisure is increasing, almost by accident. Unless there is a general return in Europe and America to the earlier oppression of industrial workers, we shall have to provide in our public policy and in our private lives for this increase and for a greater surplus of energy to be used in leisure by all those who work for a living. Already the manual and clerical workers have more spare time and more spare energy than they had fifty years ago; and—more important still—a greater variety of ways of spending leisure is available. But that is only a beginning. We must look forward. The changes of the past fifty years are worth attention chiefly because of what is coming. Is it to be a new civilization or a more unrelieved barbarism? Such a question can be answered only after a careful observation of what is actually happening. We ask, therefore, not merely how we actually do enjoy ourselves nowadays, as compared with our grandfathers, but also what sort of men and women are being produced or can be produced by our new habits outside of working hours. And the answers to such questions may be made the basis for a new civilization which is neither copied from the past nor Utopian. The actual changes in the use of leisure in the recent past will provide hints of a direction in which it is practical as well as desirable to move.

For the purpose in view, spare time or leisure must be taken in its most inclusive sense. It is understood here to include all that part of life which is not occupied in working for a living. Energy is expended and vitality grows in leisure; but in work time the direction of energy is controlled by public need or the desire for gain, whereas in leisure we are free. For a very small proportion of adult men and women, leisure is the whole of their lives. They belong to what is called the "leisured class." Some of them have retired from active work with enough income saved; and a small proportion of this "leisured class" has inherited the power to live in leisure without having done any work for a living. But the leisured classes have not been greatly affected by the changes of the past fifty years. Their position in society is no longer what it was—as the argument will show later on; but the change in their position has been mainly due to the transformation of the character of the leisure of those others who work for a living.

These others are worth most attention here. They are manual workers, clerks, bankers, teachers, shopkeepers, doctors, lawyers and—above all—women managing households or serving in them. These form the immense majority in every nation; and of that majority by far the greater part are manual workers in agriculture and industry. The spare time of these has changed in character in the past fifty years; and the changes are the first indications of a cultural revolution. This leisure is our chief subject here.

The undesired leisure of unemployment is the most urgent problem for public policy in all industrial nations. More than twenty million capable men and women who could work for a living, cannot get a living because of enforced leisure. It is generally recognized that we should be able to use their abilities and energies for the supply of the needs of all men; that problem has attracted most attention because of the obvious waste of productive power, while some people are starving, and because nobody dares to allow the unemployed to starve to death. But there is another problem of unemployment which is less obviously a problem of economics: it is the problem of the use of even such undesired leisure as that to which the unemployed are condemned. Even in a camp of prisoners of war,

THE INCREASE OF LEISURE

the problem is not merely that of escaping. There is also the problem of using such time as is available, pending escape or the conclusion of hostilities. The spare time of the millions of unemployed therefore is itself a cultural problem. That is one aspect of the leisure of those who work for a living, under modern conditions; but it is not an aspect of the problem which can be discussed here.

The great majority of those who work for a living are still employed; and the changes in their leisure are startling. First, there is more of it. In industry hours of work have decreased since 1890: in agriculture, where machinery is used, the time and, still more, the energy spent have been reduced. Household appliances, gas and electricity, better water supplies and better drainage, have lessened the the labor of millions of women, so that they can go to the movies and also keep energy to spare for other uses outside the home. The mere amount of time in hours or days which has been "saved" in the production of the same amount of goods and services would not indicate the true importance of the change. Far more important is the change in the *quality* of spare time, if men and women are not exhausted when work is over. The new hours are fuller as well as longer.

The increasing amount of spare time, however,

would have made less difference in social custom and and in mental outlook, if there had not been in the same fifty years a great increase in the number and variety of ways of using spare time. Consider the record of new leisure occupations during the past half-century. In the 1880's the bicycle had hardly come in; in the 1890's the motor-car was beginning to appear on the roads, behind the red flag of an unintended revolution! In the early 1900's the motion-picture was gradually being perfected as part of a variety entertainment; and not until about ten years ago did the radio enter into the homes of those with small incomes. Not the few rich but the millions with small incomes have been the chief beneficiaries of the new inventions and discoveries, making new uses of leisure available. Their first effect therefore has been to prevent spare time seeming empty. Those who are not rich can more easily find something to do with spare time.

A change deep down in the minds of men is implied in the new value placed upon leisure by those who work. This change will be discussed more fully later on; but it must be connected here with the increase in the amount of leisure and the increase in the ways of using it. The old proverb said that "the Devil finds work for idle hands to do." It expressed a traditional suspicion of leisure, which was natural in a world in which supplies were scanty and hard to obtain. But in our world supplies are not scanty and production can easily be increased. The old proverb is irrelevant. It is God not the Devil who must direct leisure. Other proverbial philosophy used to refer to the "busy bee"; and work, although regarded, in some moods, as a punishment for sin or as Adam's curse, in other moods was regarded as a noble duty which was worth doing for its own sake. Adam, however, never had a combined-harvester, nor even a tractor on the Five Year Plan, and the "busy bee" had not discovered chemical processes for providing scent and foodstuffs. The situation is changed. In any case it would be difficult to persuade any one but a lunatic to sacrifice the time and energy which invention and discovery have made available. There is a very general mental adjustment to the new productive system; for the increase of leisure is welcomed, not opposed. The busy bee is no longer an adequate moral guide. The butterfly is not regarded as immoral by any but the heavy-footed mind, the clod-hopper in the modern world. Spare time, if one can use it, may make life more worth living than any work time can.

Obviously the whole of a man's life cannot be dissected into leisure and work time by any clean cut of academic argument. The changes in leisure have been affected by changes in the factories and shops and offices in all industrial nations. But such occupational changes have often been discussed.[1] It will be enough here to note that instead of permitting the undesired unemployment which occurs during a period of rapidly improving machinery, the new machines and the new power supplies could be so organized as to allow the increased leisure to be more reasonably distributed. Secondly, "heavy" work has decreased both in agriculture and in industry, and therefore many of those who work in transport or engineering or on docks, for example, leave their work less exhausted than their grandfathers used to be. This is perhaps one of the reasons for the decrease in drunkenness. Thirdly, such new mechanisms as typewriters and other light machinery have greatly increased the number of paid occupations for women, which gives to great numbers of women a power to enjoy leisure not hitherto common. Even the improved preparation of foodstuffs and clothing has given greater leisure to women.

In terms of cash-returns or incomes, many sections of workers have had an improved standard of living in the past fifty years. "Real" wages have

[1] See Stuart Chase, "Men and Machines"; C. Delisle Burns, "Modern Civilization on Trial," chapter ix; Walter Meakin, "The New Industrial Revolution."

risen in many trades. But quite apart from actual rates of payment or earnings, the fall in the birth-rate in European and American countries has been great enough to cause an increase in the average family income, because smaller families involve fewer dependents on each family income. For example, the percentage of the population of Great Britain which was under four years of age went down from 13 in 1891 to 9 in 1921. The percentage of those between 45 and 64 rose from 14 in 1891 to 20 in 1921. Thus a far larger proportion of the population in modernized countries are earning incomes; and as there are fewer dependents, more is available to be spent on leisure. Also the smaller proportion of young children implies greater leisure for women.

The increase of incomes among manual workers and low-paid salary earners is due also to improved benefits from insurance against ill health, accident, or old age, to new pension-funds and to better facilities for "savings." Education and facilities for improved health may be reckoned as economic assets for those with small incomes, leaving them with more to spend upon amenities and greater skill in such expenditure. The expenditure on leisure, therefore, of those with small incomes has increased, partly because a greater number of "bare needs" are supplied "in kind" from public funds. This is an advance in civilization.

The increased amount of leisure and the new view of its importance have led to an increase in the public provision for recreation—such as libraries, parks and public baths; but this change is, no doubt, also influenced by the new education and by the demand of those to whom the franchise has recently been extended. The facilities for recreation hitherto enjoyed by those with larger incomes have been made available by the coöperative use of public funds for those with small incomes. Fox-hunting and polo are not supported by public funds: but lawn-tennis and swimming are made more generally available by such means. Indeed the expenditure of public funds on facilities for recreation may be a first sign of returning civilization, after the barbaric concentration on wealth-getting in the earlier industrial period. In former civilizations, facilities for recreation were provided by public action, as in the medieval church and in the baths of ancient Rome; and "public indigence, private wealth," as a phrase describing barbarism, was intended to refer to the absence of great public buildings, the enjoyment of which could be shared by all. We may yet have a civilization in which the facilities for recreation are more generally shared; but even their present extension implies a decisive change in the "tone" of the industrial world.

Another economic result of the increase in the purchasing power of those with low incomes is the growth of large private companies providing means for recreation—cameras, phonographs, moving pictures, and radio-sets. Fifty years ago the chief financial exploitation of the leisure-income of workers was that of the drink trade; but now the drink trade has rivals. Prostitution, a still earlier form of the business exploitation of leisure, has decreased in recent years—partly, no doubt, because of education and the new status of women, but partly also because there are so many new ways of spending spare time and energy. Even the growth of games and such sports as are supported for the sake of betting, are signs of the increased purchasing power of small incomes used in leisure. A large number of paid occupations have arisen within the last half-century owing to the new uses of leisure— for example, employment in the moving-picture industry and theaters, professional athletics, etc.; and the transport services have increased the amount of labor incidental to the crowding at sport events. Indeed "entertainment" is one of the growing industries in a world in which older services are economically depressed.

These notes of the "economic" relationships of men affected by the uses of leisure might be carried much further. Obviously the whole subject, "the economics of leisure," needs discussion, as a part of the analysis of consumption, which the traditional economic science has neglected. But the purpose of the discussion here following is the study, not of economics, but of "culture." The changes in social custom, in the tone of human intercourse, in the type of prevalent character and outlook—these are the subject-matter. The new uses of leisure are to be regarded here as important chiefly because they are forming a new kind of civilized life. That is to say, the way in which men, women, and children treat one another being different from what it was fifty years ago, new ideals are now becoming operative to affect our education, our enjoyment, and our occupations.

For the purpose of this study, the different parts of leisure must be distinguished. All time outside of work time may be divided into that part of life in which the basic needs are met and that part in which entertainment, enjoyment, or "luxury" is sought. Before discussing, therefore, what people do when they feel quite "free," it is useful to consider how far the normal conditions of their lives outside of working hours have changed recently. It is impossible to divide very clearly, for example, the use of motor-cars for going to work from their use for pleasure trips. The way in which one lives at home—whether with oil-lamps or electric light—makes a difference to one's tendency to seek entertainment elsewhere.

First, then, the new customs and habits in the everyday life of breakfast and dinner must be considered, for the new habits are signs of a mental and moral change; but they are also causes of further change. The lightening of the burden of housework, for example, is partly the result of a new social status of women; but it also promotes further change in the same direction. Within the setting of such changes the new entertainments and the other new uses of leisure are more intelligible than they would otherwise be; and many of the criticisms made in pulpits or in the press against the modern uses of leisure fail to allow sufficiently for the general change of conditions or of daily customs. Going to the movies, for example, may easily be better than what would occur if such entertainment were unavailable, in a world in which housework for women and the life of children at school have altogether changed. The whole of social life or culture in its widest sense must be recognized to have changed in the past half-century; and that change seems to point to entirely new relationships in society and entirely new standards of what is desirable, both in external conditions and in the characters of men and women.

II

THE NEW FOOD AND CLOTHING

TIME and energy to spare outside of working hours have been greatly affected in the past fifty years by changes in food and clothing. New foods and new types of clothing have provided a higher level of common comfort, favorable to a change in mental outlook, which may be described as *a greater tendency to make experiments*. Which came first—the new food and clothing or the desire to try new foods and clothes, is a futile question, like that about the hen and the egg. But clearly the change in materials and in unconsciously adopted custom is promoting a mental change in the modern world. It is this movement away from traditionalism and toward experimentalism in common life which must be studied here.

Consider first the external and obvious changes in personal habits which are due to new kinds of food and clothing. The use of these new materials easily induces men and women to live in new ways. Tradition clearly counts for much in the use of food and clothing; for men and women seldom think for themselves on such matters. They eat and wear what their parents ate and wore and in the same ways. Probably these parents copied *their* parents. But now the traditional breakfast and dinner is being transformed or abolished. Fruit is more generally eaten at all seasons; meat and cereals are less eaten. Much more tinned or canned food is available, and a greater variety from distant parts, because of the new methods of preserving food in transport. Meals are therefore tending to change their character.

For various reasons, some connected with occupations and some with leisure, there is a greater tendency to eat meals away from home. In the old days if away from home men ate in public houses or inns; and hardly any women had meals outside their own homes. But now the restaurants and tea-shops for those with small incomes have increased in number; and large companies have organized this new form of feeding, for before about 1890 such shops as those of Lyons or the A.B.C. in England or Childs in America hardly existed. The new habits have made possible more paid occupations of women. Waitresses serve the new meals; and great numbers of women can now have meals away from home, near the offices or factories. The immediate

THE NEW FOOD AND CLOTHING   19

and obvious social effect of this new method of taking food is to increase the opportunities for companionship in leisure between men and women and to make most people in city areas much more at their ease in contact or even in converse with strangers. The manners natural to meals at home are different from those which arise out of the new habits; and the new manners imply much less reserve when strangers meet. This change of attitude toward strangers carries further the social change incidental to the earlier escape from village gossip and village morality. Life in the city area made men and women into "strangers"—the new custom of taking meals away from home induces these "strangers" to meet at a new level.

The most obvious change in personal habits with regard to clothing is the increase in the use of ready-made clothes. During the past fifty years less and less of women's clothing has been made at home. Indeed to-day about ninety per cent of women's clothes are factory-made, as most men's clothes have been for a century. The variety of new materials and new colors is only just beginning to affect the "look" of the streets. But new customs have supported the changes of habit in the use of clothing. Girls with quite small incomes can now afford a variety of dresses; and young men have "sports" have; but we make experiments daily in new forms of social equality.

Some would say that this sense of equality is purchased at too high a price; because they believe that it involves the swamping of all originality or individuality in a rising tide of similar habits and customs. A second most general social effect of the new food and clothing is certainly a greater similarity of basic customs in most countries and perhaps in all the world. Even Africans on the Gold Coast now eat tinned salmon; and "national" customs are dying out, in spite of the efforts of local patriots to attract tourists. You cannot tell a butcher from a bank clerk, at least in his leisure habits; and even on the way to work, men behave in much the same way. Women also, although given to little variations in their manners as in the color or shape of their dress, are more alike than they were in the eighteenth century. Every morning in any great city area, crowds of people all behaving in the same way come out of the suburban terminals or the buses and subways. Does this make them a "mass" of precisely similar atoms—any one of which can be substituted for any other? Has "individuality" been decreased by modern conditions of dress and food and daily custom? Is human personality swamped by modern habits?

THE NEW FOOD AND CLOTHING 19

and obvious social effect of this new method of taking food is to increase the opportunities for companionship in leisure between men and women and to make most people in city areas much more at their ease in contact or even in converse with strangers. The manners natural to meals at home are different from those which arise out of the new habits; and the new manners imply much less reserve when strangers meet. This change of attitude toward strangers carries further the social change incidental to the earlier escape from village gossip and village morality. Life in the city area made men and women into "strangers"—the new custom of taking meals away from home induces these "strangers" to meet at a new level.

The most obvious change in personal habits with regard to clothing is the increase in the use of ready-made clothes. During the past fifty years less and less of women's clothing has been made at home. Indeed to-day about ninety per cent of women's clothes are factory-made, as most men's clothes have been for a century. The variety of new materials and new colors is only just beginning to affect the "look" of the streets. But new customs have supported the changes of habit in the use of clothing. Girls with quite small incomes can now afford a variety of dresses; and young men have "sports" costumes now who, in earlier days, would have had only one Sunday suit, besides their working clothes. Shorter working hours and the support given to the social side of factory and shop life have led to a greater demand for clothes suitable for dances and parties. A large number of firms now supply clothes on the basis of a weekly subscription; and there are clubs, like the old goose clubs, managed by factory workers, through which the members obtain clothes by subscription. The new materials are less durable than the old; and the tendency is toward lighter and more loosely woven woolen goods, which are cheaper. The result is a more frequent change. Clothes are not now made "to last." There is a much greater variety of colors; and new materials, such as artificial silk, are the first signs of a possible variety in the near future to supplement the traditional uses of wool and cotton.

The most general social effect of the new uses of food and clothing, taken together, is a decrease in those "caste" or "class" distinctions, which are supported by differences of dress and even by differences of meals. Clothing is one of the means for preserving distinctions in a "class" society. The early industrialism destroyed trade costumes, except in some areas for such trades as the butcher's; and nowadays most men are able to disguise themselves in their leisure as "business" men. In Russia the cloth cap of the western factory-worker has become a symbol of equality; while in the west the derby and the soft felt hat express the admiration for gentility. But in quite recent times in Europe and America, dress for all men has become less formal. Among women, the English factory girl with clogs and shawl is disappearing; at least in leisure, it is difficult to distinguish the factory-worker from the doctor's daughter. Above all, clothes in all classes of women are less heavy—which relieves the spirit as well as the body. Not very long ago only the rich could have warmth in clothing without being weighed down by shoddy material. Now light and warm materials are available for all.

In food, traditionally the rich have had variety and those who were not rich in most countries were restricted to local products. Now those with small incomes can have a choice among many different kinds of food; and because hours of work are shorter and the hours for the new forms of entertainment are the same for all, meal times tend to become the same for all social classes. The abolition of before-breakfast work and the institution of daylight saving have tended toward social equality. Thus even in daily customs, equality is in the air. Nobody knows what structure the new society will have; but we make experiments daily in new forms of social equality.

Some would say that this sense of equality is purchased at too high a price; because they believe that it involves the swamping of all originality or individuality in a rising tide of similar habits and customs. A second most general social effect of the new food and clothing is certainly a greater similarity of basic customs in most countries and perhaps in all the world. Even Africans on the Gold Coast now eat tinned salmon; and "national" customs are dying out, in spite of the efforts of local patriots to attract tourists. You cannot tell a butcher from a bank clerk, at least in his leisure habits; and even on the way to work, men behave in much the same way. Women also, although given to little variations in their manners as in the color or shape of their dress, are more alike than they were in the eighteenth century. Every morning in any great city area, crowds of people all behaving in the same way come out of the suburban terminals or the buses and subways. Does this make them a "mass" of precisely similar atoms—any one of which can be substituted for any other? Has "individuality" been decreased by modern conditions of dress and food and daily custom? Is human personality swamped by modern habits?

THE NEW FOOD AND CLOTHING

The answer is—No. It would be very original to believe that two and two make five; but no harm is done to individuality, if every one thinks they make four. When there is a separate local "magic" for every occasion, men differ more than when everybody takes quinine for fever; but individuality would not be increased by taking pounded bats and beetles. It is better to trust a doctor who is like doctors in other towns in his knowledge of medicine, than one who is so original that he knows nothing of modern science.

The idea that similar customs and beliefs destroy individuality is probably due to a mistaken conception of originality. But what makes genuine originality valuable is the possibility of seeing *more*, not mere difference from what is common. All great individuality, as contrasted with mere freakishness, is based upon a large common store of experience. The more everybody knows, the more valuable the little more that the exceptional man knows. The more everybody can do, the more valuable is that which only a genius can do. Therefore the sphere of genius or individuality is not decreased, if everybody's habits and customs become more similar. Certainly we cannot admire a society in which every one's mind is a copy of somebody else's; but those who dress alike and who think alike over a larger area of human experience can be original and "individual" as well. The pressure to think alike on all subjects is much greater in the simpler forms of society, where any variation is regarded as dangerous. The fear of originality which some critics find in America, for example, is not due to similar habits, but to the fact that society there is a composite of many racial traditions and unity is not felt to be secure. In older societies we can assume a certain unity of sentiment and belief without demanding it; and where a large amount of similarity of thought can be assumed, there is less fear of the kind of originality which is valuable. What is characteristic of the modern world is not the obvious increase in what is common but the increased possibility of variation beyond or above what is common.

In modern communities the more general similarity in dress and food expresses the higher level of common comfort and security from hunger and cold. This raising of the level does not necessarily swamp individuality; for it allows individuals to differ in what is more intimate, more essential, more subtle. Indeed it would assist clear thinking, if we could destroy the myth of the average man or "the mass" which is supposed to be in contrast with "the élite"; for there is no such thing as a "mass" of men, all indistinguishable; that idea is due to the pro-

THE NEW FOOD AND CLOTHING 25

found ignorance of common life, which scholars and critics of common folk often show.[1] To a man unaccustomed to sheep, all sheep look alike; but to a shepherd, each seems different; and so among men the more you know of common men, the more uncommon you find each to be. The supposed lack of individuality in modern conditions is an illusion of superior persons. In all societies the common element in the minds of its members is very large; and certainly modern conditions have enlarged this common element. But it is an illusion to suppose that the more common life there is, the less individuality there is. The whole thing grows: as common life grows, so individuality grows, because there is no fixed limit to human capacities. Thus dressing alike and eating the same sort of food do increase the similarity between men's minds. The area of what is common is larger; but that does *not* mean that the area of what is unique or original or individual is smaller. Both what is common and what is uncommon increase.

Similarities of dress and custom in modern life, then, do not prove that individuality is decreased; but there is positive evidence to show that individuality may be actually improved by the new con-

---

[1] The best recent statement of the point of view entirely opposed to that expressed here is in "The Revolt of the Masses," by Ortega y Gasset (tr. from Spanish, 1932).

ditions. The increase of contact with many people, which is promoted by the new customs, allows a man to be developed in many directions. To meet another man is an opportunity for bringing out in you what would otherwise lie undeveloped. And when the parts of you that "fit" into other people are developed, then you may also discover new parts of yourself, never hitherto suspected to exist. Now if people dress alike, there is not the preliminary barrier to converse, which is strangeness. If one has to overcome the shock of meeting a man in a toga or in medieval armor before one begins conversation with him, the conversation cannot go very far. But if the same man is dressed as every one else is dressed, you do not notice his dress at all. Thus the increasing similarity in the general customs of clothing and feeding provide opportunity for more varied acquaintance with people outside your own circle of occupations or outside your own place of residence. Men do not necessarily "fit," in outlook and character, with their next-door neighbors. Modern assimilation of externals allows easier approach to many outside one's immediate neighborhood; and among those outside may be some who "fit" with one's own type of mind. The greater the external similarity of habit, therefore, the greater the number of opportunities for meeting people in all classes.

The recent changes of daily custom may not have, in fact, increased the height or variety of individual insight or character. The argument does not imply that men must be more civilized, if they have more opportunities for civilization. But even if modern conditions had actually prevented the growth of individuality, it would not follow that the fault lay with these modern conditions; for the fault may be a lack of skill in the use of such opportunities. Many are still trying to make an eighteenth-century world out of twentieth-century conditions. It cannot be done. But we might try to make a twentieth-century world; and reformers might stop complaining that the world is not what it was. Of course it isn't. But it might be much better than anything that ever was.

The best way of showing clearly what might be done is to imagine a situation in which it is done. How, then, would men and women and children differ from the majority to-day, if advantage were taken generally of the new opportunities in food and clothing which have become available in the past thirty years? First, there would be less ill health and less low vitality. For example, we know that it is not good for babies in arms to drink beer; the spread of the knowledge of diet has increased the health of children and "saved" us millions of **pounds** in hospitals, in illness and mental lassitude. A savage is often less alive than a civilized man because the "supplies" for his body are often less adequate, less varied, and less certain. The more civilized a man becomes, the more alive he becomes. Mr. Chesterton's "Manalive," you remember, had too much vitality for the world he lived in. But most of us are only half alive. Clearly we need not shout and slap others on their backs to show that we are "lively"; but most of us do not perceive half of what is occurring around us, sometimes because we have traditional obstacles blocking our senses and sometimes only because our digestive processes are in such trouble. We do not see or hear or smell or taste or touch with any skill. Most people are insensitive—impercipient of what is in the rooms and streets in which they live. But some steps have been made in increasing vitality by the supply of better food and clothing.

The feeding of school-children in England began about twenty years ago as a method of supplying bare needs for a few. Now it has become an opportunity for correcting the ignorance and incompetence—and not merely the lack of income—of many. What is done on a large scale may be less skilful than an individual artist in cookery or clothing can make it; but artists of that sort are not

THE NEW FOOD AND CLOTHING

many and few of them are women. Large-scale cooking in schools and restaurants is often better than what is done at home. Ready-made clothing is often better than home-made misfits. But the low vitality of many is due to ignorance of diet and of the art of cooking in their homes, which is corrected when better brains than the family happens to possess are used for the preparation of food and the supply of clothing.

Consider, again, the change which might be effected by a more skilful use of clothing. The new world might be less burdened by clothes. We could rid ourselves of more than half of what we carry about. The weight of the old materials might be replaced by a few light and yet equally warm pieces —frequently changed, perhaps destroyed after use and never washed. In better warmed houses less clothing would be required. Fashions would be more varied, more changeable and, to old-fashioned eyes, more fantastic. Color would come back into men's clothing. Each person would have many different kinds of garments for different occupations or simply for the pleasure of change. All these new opportunities are in our hands and the results of using them skilfully would be to increase the vitality of men, women, and children—to decrease the "dead weight" of trivial illnesses, of inertia in mind and body from which we still suffer. It is true that in modern times we have got rid of the gross diseases, cholera, typhus, and leprosy; but we have only just begun to be civilized. We do not have among us the ghastly sights—the lepers and cripples and lunatics—which hung about the streets and churches of the Middle Ages; but the opportunities we have are not yet fully used—as one can see by looking at the way in which people walk or talk or move their hands or use their eyes or ears. Greater skill in such simple arts as cooking and wearing clothes would produce a new type of men and women.

Those who have absorbed their "culture" from books may be annoyed at all this talk about food and clothing; but the problems involved are as important as those of birth-control or proportional representation or "the new poetry." When Athens became civilized, there was a flood of little books published there on diet. The French are more civilized than some other nations who shall be nameless, because .they know that food and drink are not mere "fuel." When people can think freely and act skilfully with regard to their food and clothing, then it will be reasonable to believe that they are "up to the game" of a social transformation. But whatever the future use of the new opportunities

THE NEW FOOD AND CLOTHING   31

may be, even to-day new habits, largely unconscious, increase the vitality of thousands of men and women. Eating in tea-shops, wearing clothes like the best observable, taking fruit instead of bacon—all this, which has come about in the past thirty years, made men and women different from what they were, increased the range of their perceptions and improved their ability in social intercourse.

Obviously cause and effect are interwoven here as in other parts of one's experience. The new customs would never have appeared, if there had not been, since about 1900, a new education—much more skilful, much more interesting to the pupils and much less "bookish." Also women for the first time in history, during the past thirty years, have been more generally and more skilfully educated. This has interacted with the new transport and the new system of production to increase the desire for new kinds of food and clothing and the use of them in all social classes. The result is a higher common level and greater vitality for each, even if it is only the bare beginning of a new age.

The most important social change, however, of the past fifty years is the increase in the tendency to make experiments in common life. The number of those who are actually making experiments in diet and in daily life at home may still be small; but their influence is likely to be reinforced by recent economic tendencies. Economic "booms" and "depressions" compel many, who would otherwise never think about such things, to change their everyday customs. And indeed the whole tendency of "consumption" in the past half-century has been toward greater variety of possible choice in food and clothing. The opportunity for change in habits has played into the hands of those who have the experimental rather that the imitative type of mental "set" or attitude. Probably in every generation there are some people of this sort. They are the heretics of common life. Perhaps indeed there is in every man something of a heretic and something of a traditionalist; but the whole of our education has hitherto aimed at suppressing the heretical tendency in common folk; and the result has been a society in which social psychologists have been able to find only the laws of imitation, not the stir of imaginative reasoning which distinguishes civilization from barbarism. Make common folk, by economic pressure and obsolete educational methods, into members of a mob; and then there is evidence enough of the mob-mind or the crowd-mind. Social scientists then take the results of barbarism for the nature of the human being in society.

But a new age is beginning. In the past fifty

THE NEW FOOD AND CLOTHING 33

years there has been a lightening of the tone, a brightening of the air, in the ordinary life of breakfast and dinner. It is as if the stuffy clothes and meals of an earlier time had had a dose of air and sun. It is not assumed that it is better to have more opportunities; for whether it is better or worse depends upon the ability of actual men and women to use what is to hand. A savage may have no use for a library. The new situation, therefore, may be considered to be a collection of tools for civilized life; and education should leave us with knowledge and skill for living, in the simplest sense of the word living, that is, in the way we eat our food and clothe ourselves. Now there are already many small books on diet, which have a large popular sale. There is a very general interest in the new theory of vitamins. There are schools for the scientific study of diet and the treatment of food; and in a growing number of elementary schools there is some attention paid to the improvement of skill in diet—traditionally still confined to girls—as if boys did not eat! In clothing, the new tendencies are not yet carried so far; but there are "movements" for reform in clothing, and the beginnings of a scientific study of the beauty and utility of new materials and new shapes for clothes.

All this implies a willingness to think of change in

food and clothing. That is experimentalism. It may effect a social change of outlook, going far beyond breakfast and dinner; for if daily habits remain traditional, no industrial or political reorganization is possible; but if the daily habits of a great number of common folk are changing, a traditional system of industry and politics can hardly survive. Greater skill in the use of the new opportunities in daily life will form a type of mind that is useful in public affairs in a time of fundamental industrial change. But the skill in new habits, in the use, for example, of tinned food and artificial silk, has already spread further than most economists and political scientists seem to know; and the experimentalism in common life has already undermined the security of old habits and attitudes in the whole social system. Recent changes in food and clothing are clearly unsettling old customs; but these changes are experiments in new customs. And the minds or characters of modern men and women, therefore, tend to be less fixed or rigid and more open to new ideas —not only in food and clothing. New customs make men and women "new," not merely because they do what their grandparents did not do, but chiefly because their attitude is changed.

The existence of new customs increases the tendency of the new generation to make experiments

THE NEW FOOD AND CLOTHING

in new ways of living—new ways of meeting people, new attitudes toward common things, new subjects of conversation, and new phases of friendship. Besides, openness of mind makes it easier for people to meet those who differ from them in opinion or outlook or attitude; and less oppressive surroundings make both men and women more lively. In the old days, for example, women were oppressed by the traditional necessities of food and clothing, the provision of which was chiefly in their hands in most households. Now women are freer. They are easier to meet on other levels than that of gossip. But it is not necessary to say whether the new situation is actually better in its effects. The only certain result of recent change in food and clothing is the increase in the tendency to make experiments.

III

THE HOME IN THE MODERN WORLD

THE tendency to make experiments in the customs of everyday life has affected very greatly the modern attitude toward the home. As material instruments, the house and its furnishings are treated more freely; and as a complex of human relationships, the home is now undergoing a subtle transformation, even among those who would by no means be called "modern." The external changes and the changes in personal relationships are both parts of one movement; but for the purpose here in view, the material changes may be considered first.

In order to discover what difference the past fifty years have made to that part of leisure which is ordinary life at home, it would be best for the reader to attempt his own analysis of what is under his nose. Look first at the room you are sitting in and at its contents. What is the color of the walls? What are the colors and shapes of the furniture? How many "pictures" and other traditional ornaments are on the walls? If you are in some European country, there is probably a magic spot in the room, in front of a fireplace—a medieval survival—and over the fireplace an ancient shelf laden with peculiar traditional objects like a savage's private charms. Most of the chairs in the room are probably traditional in design, and so designed as to make people feel inclined to rise out of them as soon as possible. The comfortable chairs can hardly be moved at all; and the light chairs are in danger of going to pieces —for it is still not probable that you use steel and canvas to sit in. When you have made a survey of the room, to find out how much is traditional and how much modern, you should then observe the customs of the local people—in order to discover any signs that the Middle Ages have ended, not only in the furniture but in the way the members of your household treat one another.

Not many live differently at home from the way in which people of a similar age and position lived fifty years ago. Millions have not changed, because they cannot. They have neither time nor money nor opportunity for changing their home or their habits. But many more could change than actually do. Even those who go into the new housing areas of the past ten years take the old ornaments and the old manners with them. But some few have changed;

and some small changes have been made even in the lives of the majority. These are the first signs of a new kind of home in the modern world.

If, in spite of all the opportunities which modern mechanisms and modern attitudes of mind imply, the changes are so few and so small—that is due largely to the defects of our educational tradition; and these defects are more serious than the shortness of school life for the majority or the too great crowding of class-rooms. Education is still too "literary." We are taught to read print, not to see color—to know the names of the rivers of Spain, not to notice the shape of the tables we use. We learn to add up figures, not to measure chairs, nor even to move them skilfully; still less to decide whether they are beautiful or not. The color of most school-rooms is abominable and the furniture hideous; but nobody is supposed to notice it. The lecture-rooms at universities might be less like prison-cells; but there are professors who would be ashamed of praising the wrong author, who have no feeling at all about the walls that oppress the spirit in the dungeons in which they make their comments on dead theories. Some men and women claiming to be educated, never notice at all the rooms they live in, the furniture, or the shapes of the forks and spoons they use. Their education has

THE HOME IN THE MODERN WORLD 39

blinded them to ugliness; and it is not considered worse for that reason. They are the "cultured" and "upper" classes, not merely sons and daughters of dock laborers and textile workers; and they are very kindly extending the education in blindness and deafness to those whom they still call the "lower" classes.

With such an education it is not to be wondered at that most European houses are what they were fifty years ago; but some have changed. This change is to be seen best in Germany and Holland. In the new housing areas, great blocks of buildings, as in Vienna, as well as lines of small houses, as in Frankfurt, embody the new principles of space and air and light. New materials are replacing brick. Glass is more skilfully used. Electricity for lighting and heating, as in the new workers' flats in the St. Pancras area of London, and oil-furnaces, as in the United States—all these are only the beginnings of a new form of house. Social habits are local still; and they differ sometimes because of traditional attitudes toward one's fellows. A few years ago I was at a conference in Holland between a few molders and fitters, railwaymen, and textile workers —rank and file trade-unionists, from five or six different countries. The discussion turned upon the sort of houses the public authorities ought to build.

The British in the conference, even the women, were in favor of small separate houses, each with a tiny strip of garden, its own kitchen, and its own place for washing clothes. The Germans, Austrians, Dutch, and Scandinavians were all in favor of large buildings with flats, but containing also large common eating-halls and recreation rooms, common cooking and common laundry arrangements. They said that this was not only a cheaper plan but also it allowed finer architecture and, best of all, it gave women more freedom from cooking and washing. The difference between those two points of view is largely traditional. It reflects the difference in men's minds as to the place of what is private and what is public in everyday life. But no doubt differences as to the desirable structure of the house are partly due to differences of climate. In Continental countries the cold of winter necessitates a steam-heating plant or at least stoves more efficient than the British coal fire. And yet the new conditions of work and the opportunities offered by new inventions will probably change habits in all countries. The home, as an apparatus for everyday life, will always differ in different countries: but all countries may have new types of house.

Modern standards applied to the house imply that we require from it at least warmth and shelter and the intimacy which is dependent upon dignity or beauty. The whole thing is merely an instrument —half mechanism and half work of art, for everyday use. The new opportunities made available in the past fifty years have hardly begun to be used in many countries. Skill in ventilation ought to permit the use of better windows and doors. New colors might make walls less prison-like. New forms of building material, to replace or to improve the brick which we still use in England as it was used 6,000 years ago, might make the whole house less damp and cold. But what is now needed is a more general recognition that a house should not be what houses have hitherto been and certainly not a copy of any other house. The possibilities are innumerable. Electricity, for example, can supply not only light and heat but also—as in American cities—vacuum-cleaners, electric baths, telephones, radio-sets and—the latest invention—a window-box which lets in the air and keeps out the noise of the streets. Plainly we are at the beginning of a new period in the history of the house as an instrument or work of art for everyday use.

A few are beginning to think freely and less traditionally about their houses. They are asking questions about what nobody used even to consider, because it all seemed so obvious. For example, what is a window for? Is it for light? Then why curtains? Is it for air? Then why are many windows impossible to open? Which is most important—the wall or the window? These questions are being asked by increasing numbers of younger folks. Mr. H. G. Wells a long time ago wrote that we had not made as much progress in designing our houses as in designing our battle-ships; but perhaps now at last it is possible to hope for a house as practical as a battleship. Old houses may still remain, because of the capital cost of replacing them; but just as the most modern hospitals and schools are so built as to be replaced in thirty years, so perhaps we shall treat houses as tents for us nomads of the new world. And as with the house, so with the household appliances—chairs, tables, forks, and spoons—they might be better, if we were willing to think what such appliances are for. They are not forces of nature which we cannot control; but most of us never think of them at all—that is to say, we accept our grandmothers' designs.

The effect of recent changes in the house and its furniture can already be seen in the lives of men, women, and children in their homes. Men's minds and their attitudes toward other men are changed by the circumstances in which they live. The things which surround you, in the place where you live, affect the way in which you act and think. Even forks and spoons reflect particular types of manners. Chopsticks belong to ancestor worship. The traditional view of life indeed supposes these things to be only scenery among which our noble selves may act as characters in the piece; but such a view is mistaken. All the world may be a stage; but the things on the stage are not merely scenery. They are characters. In Maeterlinck's play, "The Blue Bird," sugar and bread and water had voices and characters of their own. There is some truth in the idea. The spoon you eat with has a "mind of its own," as can be seen when a baby tries to make it go into its mouth; and when one has mastered the spoon, then it seems to have none of that "cussedness" which shows character. If you look closely, however, at the whole complicated machine which is the house you live in and its furniture and other tools for living, you will see that the new things in it, like the old things, are "characters," in the sense that they play upon your character. They have "parts" in the play. If we change from oil-lamps to electricity for lighting, the labor of women is changed and probably also the temper of those who used to search for the matches in the dark and cut the smoking wick. The modern house is likely to make more civilized men and women and children, because it is cleaner, lighter, more airy, more spacious, and less traditional, therefore more easily changed so as to suit those who live in it. The change of the past fifty years—even such very moderate change as is implied in the new housing areas in Great Britain—has given more people light and air and space at home. But we have hardly begun to use the opportunities already available.

It is not denied, however, that the chief characters in the home are human. The changes of the past thirty years have affected these also. Men and women and children are beginning to use the home in new ways. In the first place, they tend to change more often from home to home. Men are less "stuck" in one corner than they used to be. Again, it is only a few who have completely changed; but it must be remembered that, apart from the adventurous type who used to emigrate or go homeless, the vast majority have always lived not merely where they were born but where their grandparents were born; and not merely in the same town or part of the country, but in the same house. In some countries, such as France, this continues to be true about almost everybody; but in Great Britain and still more in America, many more people change their dwelling from place to place during a few years. Our house becomes less like a cave and more like a tent. We are becoming, in a new sense, nomadic.

Again, people belonging to the same household who are affected by the modern conditions of living, see less of one another than in the old days. Perhaps in a few years a really "modern" wife will say to a really "modern" husband—when the husband comes home— "What! You here again!" Probably the modern husband will not be so much surprised to see his wife at home; but of course he will assume that the place of the woman is *not* in the home. As for the children, when they can walk, the parents may be quite uncertain when they will see them again.

At one time the dwelling-place was the center for the whole of one's life. There the work was done; there the meals were eaten; there the children picked up what knowledge they could; and there everybody always slept. Sleeping seems to be the only thing that every one still does in the place he calls his home. Schools and factories and offices are already comparatively old-fashioned; and all these take people away from home. But clubs and recreation grounds and moving pictures are new; and these scatter the family even more. The increase in ease of transport makes people look upon home as little more than a dormitory; but still, if asked where you "live," you probably give the address of the place where you only sleep, because in the old days you would really have "lived" there. Nobody quite likes to say that he lives in about half a dozen different places; and so, just as we say the sun rises although we know perfectly well that it doesn't, so we say we live where we only sleep. Everybody has left home for all other purposes.

On the basis of this tendency one can go farther into the future. There are some remnants of an earlier social structure which will probably disappear. For example, the nineteenth century produced the distinction between the part of a city in which the rich live and that in which the poor live. The rich literally fled from the crowding which early industrialism produced, largely because the new wealth-making process produced squalor and barbarism of manners. The gin-shops and the tenements made the slums; and the rich made "the West End" the substitute for an upper-class paradise. But under modern conditions, this division is obsolete. Those with smaller incomes are not more ill-mannered or uneducated; still less are they diseased or drunk. We may therefore see an unconscious disappearance of the class divisions in the streets we inhabit. The poor man may live with ease next-door to the rich; and the scholar next-door to any of the other servants of the community—the policeman, the postman or the engineer. So much education and public health have already effected. But we still think of a "home" as if it were by itself and not in a group of houses of a certain economic or social class.

A house, in fact, is part of the common dwelling-place for a community. The greater separateness of the members of a household—their finding of occupations and interests outside their own house—is accompanied by a growth of groups or communities for this or that purpose. But here we find one of the most glaring defects in the new housing areas of the local authorities especially in Great Britain. Most of them have been designed as groups of boxes for sleeping in; and when the area is large enough, a school, perhaps, has been added and some religious bodies have set up churches. But most of these new housing areas are without any soul of their own and have no place for a common soul. There is no common meeting place; for most housing reformers are still living on the nineteenth century conception of houses as separate sleeping-boxes without any place in a common setting. They have no conception of a dwelling-place for a whole community, with a common life of work or at least of leisure; and it would be considered to be "waste," if any public money were spent upon a public building for the enjoyment of the community. Most modern houses are small, because most incomes are small. But it does every one good to feel the great space of a noble hall and to see architecture at its greatest serving him. This sense of space and light in the old days was satisfied by the great medieval church in the little town or village; for the church building was not merely a place for worship or preaching, but also a general meeting place for all the common life. And now it is pathetic to see in the villages of Great Britain the empty shells of these great spaces for the common life, which were once full of color and the sound of voices. But they belong to a vanished age. What we need now, to make the home part of a civilization, is a new form of what the Middle Ages found in its church buildings—space and noble proportions and the best in all the arts of the age, for the use of the whole of a community. Such places are being built here and there; in America the school-house in new towns is often the noblest building in the place, where the grown-ups go for their dances and their concerts and debates on public affairs, when the children are in bed. When a community vigorously desires to live a common life, it will produce its own building; and the quality of the life it desires will be seen in the quality of the building it produces. But so far little has been done to make the modern setting in a community for the modern home.

Such changes, however, as have occurred in our attitude toward the home we live in imply both a much greater use of new appliances in it and a much greater tendency to leave it—which points to the coming of a new kind of community.

We may now consider the new relationships between the members of the household themselves. In every civilization there are differences of intimacy between its members; and it may be assumed that we are going to develop further on the lines of monogamy and the small family of children living with their parents. How then will the two relationships be affected—that of the wife and husband and that of the parents and children? It is implied, in what has just been said about the home as a part of a community, that no wife is, in the modern world, only or mainly a wife and no husband is only or mainly a husband. Unless each is interested and, in fact, devoted to something else, each will "bore" the other. If the husband's job is merely to make money for his wife and family, he is a caveman with a lair. The modern man serves the community in what he does; that, not what he makes out of it, is his excuse or justification for sitting about in buses and filling up space in an office or a workshop. And the wife, even if her work is at home, has other ways of sharing the life of her time. But the change in the attitude toward the work one does for a living is very slow.

In leisure at any rate, in the modern family both husband and wife tend to find entertainment outside the home. The movie and the motor-bus have made that possible. Whether the radio has had a contrary effect, is not yet clear. It may keep people more at home; but if it does, when they stay at home to listen, they talk to one another much less and, in any case their minds are fixed upon what is far outside their home. You can travel farther from home with the radio than you can by going to a theater. In any case, home life is less absorbing. Again, the management of the house, which is generally in the hands of the wife, takes less of her time and energy, in these days of gas-cooking and electric light; and the children are fewer and better cared for at school. Therefore there is more opportunity for the wife to be an equal of her husband, in the amount and the uses of leisure, in her interests and activities. To put it in blunt words, fewer women need be slaves in homes. The relationship therefore of husband and wife will be radically altered; not perhaps in affection or sentiment, but in actual habits of life—in the way in which the life of one affects the life of the other. Equality is more possible to-day; even if this new equality is so far only, as John Stuart Mill said— "Reciprocal superiority in which each has in turn the enjoyment of leading and being led."

The other relationship in the home is that of parents to children. Every one knows that there are, in general, fewer children in each family than there were in 1900; but also the schools have changed, so that nowadays the child looks forward to school time and feels an interest in what he learns. The movie has given to children a new interest outside the home, thus increasing their ability to live lives of their own. The result is that the relationship of parents to children is different from what it was fifty years ago; for nowadays it is only one of many important relationships of the child, even if it remains the most important. The further result may be that parents will less and less be taken as guides or models by their children; and that, some think, will be better. Modern parents do not admire themselves so much as to compel their children to be like themselves. Fifty years ago many parents had not themselves been to school; now we are in the first generation of a civilized life in which all have had some education. The result is a greater intelligence on the part of parents, with regard to the place of the school in the child's life. The parent recognizes that he or she has a part of the task of education; but most of the task is carried on outside the home. The child therefore in modern conditions is much less dependent upon the home.

A second change in the relationship of parent and child is the more general recognition that this relationship ends at adolescence. It is very difficult for some parents to grasp that Tom and Mary, who were once children, cease to be children and must not be spoken to or treated as children after adolescence. The inevitable friction arising from the lack of recognition of adolescence leads girls and boys to desire to leave home as soon as they can. But in the modern world parents can recognize when children cease to be children. In modern conditions, no one ought to be treated as a child after about fifteen years of age; and therefore the problem for parents is how to make certain that the dependent child of former years shall be the equal companion of later years. But success in making that change in the form of intimacy obviously depends partly upon the intelligence of the parents, partly upon the kind of education the child is receiving. Perhaps indeed the modern relationship of parents and children will create a new type of intimacy, as different from the patriarchy of early times as the intimacy of a modern husband and wife is different from the charming but somewhat simple-minded "love" of the young people who in the old days used to "get married and live happily ever after." The intimacy of the child and the parent is necessarily limited; it is often exhausted during the adolescence of the child; it is always destroyed by any attempt at superior airs on the part of the parent when adolescence is over. But here again "ripeness is all." Skill in managing a very difficult situation can be acquired, even by parents and children; but how much of that skill is promoted by the education of to-day, it would be impolite to inquire. Most education seems to be devoted to a knowledge of things; and very few educationalists seem to see that the discovery of personalities that will "go" with ours and the development of intimacy with them, is the highest of all tasks. Indeed even education in the so-called humanities seems to be more concerned with dead men and their works than with the people with whom one's life has to be passed.

Changes in modern life and leisure seem to occur too quickly for our educational system and its methods to keep pace with them. From one point of view acquiescence in traditional household customs and in the old-fashioned home is disappearing; largely because of new ways of using leisure and because children as well as adults are less dependent upon the other members of their household for their interests. But from another point of view, a new kind of community is growing up, in which the home is only one and not the most important part. Like all social changes, the change in the attitude toward home and family, at least among a few, is distressing to old people; and obviously the change is not welcomed generally. But it is not due to any new theory or gospel; it is the effect of new occupations, of the motor-bus, the movies, and the radio. The change is probably inevitable. We can guide it in one direction or another; but we cannot stop it. Hence the importance of imaginative intelligence for overcoming the difficulties in the use of increased leisure and for promoting those new forms of intimacy between persons, which will be most enduring and most vital under modern conditions. Social intercourse is more fluid now than it was fifty years ago. The home is subtly changing in its relationship to the world outside and the members of the household are in new relationships, one to the other.

IV

THE SOCIAL EFFECTS OF MOTOR-CARS

WE CAN move faster and farther and with greater ease than our grandfathers could. The motor-car within the past half-century has become a rival to the railway; and its daily use is already affecting our mental attitude toward time and distance. We are passing into a new form of civilization of wider spaces and fuller time.

Part of the social effect of the new mechanisms for travel and transport is due to their use in the productive system—that is to say, in what has been called above our work time. Men and women live farther from their work and are within easier reach of it, because of the motor-bus and the private car. But the social effects of the motor-car is greatest in its use for the enjoyment of leisure. Travel has become commoner and its range, for millions of those with small incomes, has been extended by motor tours.[1]

[1] The aëroplane has begun to carry the same change further; and the aëroplane clubs of to-day, although still for the rich, are forerunners of a new extension of travel which will, no doubt, occur as the cost of aëroplane journeys decreases.

For the purpose here in view, however, it is unnecessary to distinguish the leisure uses of the new travel-machines from their other uses. Their social effect is to be seen in the same change of mental outlook which results both in leisure and in work time from the new experience of motion. Indeed the whole temper of our age, as distinguished from that of fifty years ago, may be understood by comparing the contrast between the two periods to the contrast between the outlook of the agricultural laborer and of the sailor. The agricultural laborer looks to the ground he stands on and the make of the earth as far as the plow will travel in a day's work. But the sailor looks to the horizon; for the place he is in never interests him as much as the place he is going to. If these two kinds of outlook are taken to be typical of two civilizations, we may be said to be passing now from the civilization of the land under our feet to that of the horizon—from the civilization of stability to that of movement. That is perhaps reading too much into the motor-car and the aëroplane; but in so far as they have made a difference to men's minds, the difference is that they extend the area of the world which is familiar; they make the agricultural laborer into a seaman. What then are the strange

SOCIAL EFFECTS OF MOTOR-CARS

voyages upon which we are now embarked? Where are we going so fast and so far?

Of all the uses of the internal-combustion engine, its use in the motor-bus and the private motor-car have had the most general effect upon all sorts of people. First, the number of people who use motor-cars and buses every day for going to work or for pleasure, is increasing rapidly. Again, the experience of driving the new engines is much more widespread than locomotive driving could be. And further, with the motor, the road has come back to its own as one of the chief instruments of civilization. Historians say that Rome civilized Europe and ancient Britain by her roads. Those roads made control possible; but more important still, they made trading easier between distant peoples; and men learned—until the Roman roads fell into decay—that strangers were not necessarily enemies. Perhaps, after nearly two thousand years, the road will again unite the European peoples and make the British less insular. One can imagine great motor routes, running throughout the Continental mass which is made up of Europe and Asia, on which routes there would be no frontiers, because any motors using them would be internationalized by common rules. Already it is announced that a great motor road from Calais to Constantinople is being built.

A century ago Mr. Creevey wrote from Knowsley on November 14th 1829— "I had the satisfaction, for I can't call it pleasure, of taking a trip of five miles in the locomotive machine, which we did in just a quarter of an hour—that is, twenty miles an hour! As accuracy upon this subject was my great object, I held my watch in my hand at starting and all the time; and as it has a second hand, I knew I could not be deceived; and so it turned out, there was not the difference of a second between the coachee or conductor and myself. But observe, during those five miles, the machine was occasionally made to put itself out or *go it;* and then we went at the rate of twenty-three miles an hour, and just with the same ease as to motion or absence of friction as the other reduced pace. But the quickest motion is to me *frightful;* it is *really flying* and it is impossible to divest yourself of the notion of instant death to all upon the least accident happening. It gave me a headache which has not left me yet. Sefton is convinced that some damnable thing must come of it. . . . Altogether I am extremely glad indeed to have seen this miracle and to have travelled in it. Had I thought more of it than I do, I should have had the curiosity to try it; but having done so, I am quite satisfied with my first achievement being my *last*."

Sixty years later, about 1890, is Beeching's poem on going downhill on a bicycle:

> Swifter and yet more swift;
> Till the heart with a mighty lift
> Makes the lungs laugh, the throat cry—
> "O bird see; see bird I fly.
>
> Is this, is this your joy?
> O bird, then I, though a boy
> For a golden moment share
> Your feathery life in air."

Now, if going twenty-three miles an hour in a train and going downhill on a bicycle are like flying, what is flying like? The new generation will be already accustomed to speed. They will not think a "bird's-eye-view" the highest obtainable or a "bee-line" or "as the crow flies" the fastest or the straightest road.

But there are other effects of the recent change in the means of going about. The motor-car has come into general use only in the past thirty years; and already a new type of human outlook and human character has been developed by it. The figures to show the increase of motor traction and the decrease of horse traffic can be easily observed.

Men in cities are being farther separated from domesticated animals and those who can manage animals are fewer. Street accidents have increased; but the number of people in the streets has also increased. Indeed the nature and use of streets and roads have changed; for nowadays streets and roads are passages to far lands, not places for gossip or selling goods. People move about more swiftly, more easily and far more frequently. They are accustomed to changing from place to place. Again, the motor-bus has carried further the division of the home from the work place. Consider for example, the daily experience of millions in going and coming from work—or in the case of women who work at home, their usual method of shopping. Or consider the distance from home or work place to the place for entertainment. The new situation, which began about thirty years ago, is not due to the suburban train. That may be as old as about 1860. The new situation is the result of the motor-bus.

The census for Great Britain in 1931 gave some interesting information about the changed distribution of the population. The flow from the country into the towns, which had continued until 1921, has ceased in the past ten years. That is to say, the proportion of people living under urban conditions remains the same as it was about ten years ago. But a new change is occurring in the distribution of people in the towns themselves. The small towns are becoming smaller and the large towns larger. One in every five inhabitants of England and Wales lives in London: one in every five of the inhabitants of Scotland lives in Glasgow; Liverpool and Manchester have grown larger in ten years; and small towns such as Nelson, Accrington, and Darwen, have become smaller. This is mainly due, of course, to a change in the character of industry; but it is due in part to the new transport system. The greater the distance separating the home from the work place or the shop, the larger the concentration of population which is possible. In the London area, men who lose their jobs in North London, can work at jobs in South London without changing their homes. The London University Colleges and the University of Glasgow draw their students, most of whom live at home, from increasingly distant districts. The longer the distance over which it is easy to go in search of entertainment, the more entertainment is found in huge city areas. The same concentration is happening in Germany, France, and the United States; and therefore the change from small town to city area cannot be due only to the changes which are characteristic of British industry. It is plainly more possible now to sleep far away from the place at which one works or at which one finds entertainment; and this, as it was pointed out in the last chapter, makes a great difference to what people think of their homes. In any case a greater number than ever before have the daily experience of work and of entertainment at a distance from their homes.

Another effect of the daily use of motors is familiarity with a larger "circle" round one's dwelling. Especially in rural areas, the use of motor-buses has released the farm worker and the villager from dependence upon his immediate neighbors. This has injured the small shopkeeper in villages; and it has been an advantage to the shops and the movies in larger towns. But more important than such economic consequences is the fact that it has released men and still more women from the village-pump gossip, which used to be their only entertainment. It has made visits to the town movies possible, even for those who work on farms. It has opened up the minds of those who would otherwise spend their spare time in their Sunday clothes gaping in the lanes or in the village streets.

Another social effect of the new transport is due to the fact that in motor-buses and street-cars, as in some suburban trains, there are no "classes." All passengers pay the same fare and have the same kind of comfort or discomfort. People with very different homes and very different occupations, sit side by side. The motor-bus is therefore one of the causes of the increasing similarity of dress. People copy what seems to them to be best; and they see something new to copy more often than in old days. Obviously motor-buses could not be used, if men carried swords and women wore trains to their dresses. I can remember the days of the hat-pin in the bus; but happily disarmament has been achieved in women's hats; and, in spite of attempts by the dress designers, I cannot believe that women will ever wear sweeping skirts again, if they are to use the motor-bus. But any one who looks round him at ordinary things must be struck by something deeper down than similarity of dress. That is the similarity of manners, which has been shown in a former chapter to be partly due to changes in food and clothing. The new common manners are due also to the daily mixing of all sorts in buses. Even walking along a pavement in a city is a skilled job —as you will discover if you try to make out how it is that you "steer" along the pavement to avoid collisions. But getting in and out of a bus requires a new sort of skill; and the way in which you pay your fare—your manners to your fellow-passengers and to the bus conductor—all this is typical of the modern world. But when the motor-bus brought all sorts of very different people into continual close contact, it leveled up the tone of manners. There is much less of an air of superiority and condescension among passengers than there used to be, when only a few could avoid walking. There is a much more general assumption of equality of status in the manner of each man to the others; and the attitude of men to women and of women to men is less sentimental than it used to be and much more that of equals. Here then is the basis of a new kind of democracy, not dependent upon voting, nor upon the assertion of rights. It is a new form of social intercourse—based upon good manners between equals.

All the social effects so far noted, however, are less fundamental than the general change of mental attitude toward speed. The slow-moving generations of walkers or horsemen moved slowly also in their minds. Society was less flexible, when time seemed to be of no account because its flow was regular and most of it was "empty." Now only a rustic waits for the lines of passing omnibuses to end: *rusticus expectat dum defluat omnibus*. Obviously the locomotive and the steamship began

SOCIAL EFFECTS OF MOTOR-CARS 65

this transformation in the sense of time; for men gave up what had been the traditional virtue of waiting, when they no longer depended upon wind and weather for the length of time on their journeys. But a far greater number have been affected intimately by the motor-car so as to understand the varieties of speed; and the aëroplane is already carrying further our capacity for realizing different rates of motion.

There is a pleasure in mere speed; and there is pleasure also in feeling the power to go at many different speeds. Indeed perhaps the sense of greatly different rates of speed is new to human beings.[2] Mr. Creevy in 1829 felt twenty-three miles an hour to be an extreme limit of speed; but many motorists have been at eighty miles an hour on a road; and we all know that that is far too slow for an aëroplane. Already a speed of four hundred and eight miles an hour has been achieved. Clearly we shall have to furbish up the old poetic phrase about "the twinkling of an eye" or "swift as thought." Eyes do not twinkle so very fast, not even the eyes of moving-picture stars; and thought is as slow as digestion, if boiled potatoes do not stop our thinking altogether. Speed is comparatively new in its effect on

[2] It may be suggested that the modern philosophical conception of space-time as a unit and the modern conception of relativity are both results of the experience of the new travel-machines.

the mind, and we do not yet know what the effect is; but clearly a change is occurring in the prevalent outlook upon time and distance.

It may be held, however, that it is not speed which has had the greatest social effect in our time, but merely changing from place to place; and that may lead nowhere. Civilized life may be destroyed by the *superficiality*, which is due to the ease with which uneducated people can travel; for superficiality is the glance and the blurred vision and dulled hearing of those who pass by. The man who passes along the road so fast that he cannot tell an oak from a beech or a grocery from a butcher's shop, is not "seeing the world." He is missing all but its surface. It is good to be able to pass from place to place easily and quickly, if there is any sufficient reason for leaving one place or going to another; but if places become only points on a mileometer, there is no reason for going anywhere, however fast you go. You cannot know a place unless you have let it soak into you at many hours of the day and night, in many lights, in many weathers; and therefore rushing from place to place does not increase one's knowledge of places. The result may be superficiality of mind. The same danger of superficiality lies even in the motor or the train which takes you and thousands of others, whom you know by sight, every day backward and forward. Knowing people by sight is not knowing *people* but only their clothes and their ridiculous faces. What is behind the face may be worse, but at any rate it is different; and you can't know much of that by merely traveling in the same bus or the same suburban train with a familiar face. But the result of this modern habit of travel in masses is the *lack of real intimacy,* from which so many of the inhabitants of the great city areas suffer. It is an old saying that a man may be lonely in a crowd; and clearly the mere presence of innumerable others, having no intercourse with him, may make a man superficial in his human relationships. The evil of such a superficiality may be best understood, if we allow for the fact that each man lives at many different levels. A part of him lies below what the psychologists call "the level of consciousness"; a part of him is employed in such semi-conscious action as walking or putting on his hat. Another part, at a higher level, is that with which he sees and hears what surrounds him; and another part attempts to manipulate the outer world to his desires. Now men meet at different levels. The more intimate the conversation, the higher the level from which both parties to the conversation view the universe. Love is not blind. It does not always see what is under its nose, because its eyes are on the horizon; but it sees more than hate sees and much more than indifference can. The majority of those, however, who travel daily in crowds do not come into intimate contact with any one. They treat another person as only something which fills a seat in the bus or the train. They pass over London Bridge in the same swarm day after day; and each individual of the swarm becomes, even in his or her own mind, only something that shoves or dodges other persons. The result is a superficiality, which cannot occur in a village—where every one really knows every one else; and this is the effect of the new system of transport in buses and trains.

As for the new travel by air, the number of those who have personal experience of such travel is much less in Great Britain than in Germany or in America. But everywhere, at least through the newspapers, we are being influenced by aëroplane journeys to India or round the world. The old conception of the skies is changed. A man who had traveled for a while in an aëroplane, which had turned upside down, told me that he looked over the side and saw the sky and looked over his head and saw the earth. Again, the range of our acquaintance with the weather has been extended mainly

SOCIAL EFFECTS OF MOTOR-CARS

for use by aëroplanes. The traveler by air needs to know what sort of weather it is five hundred miles away. But here again the "spread" of knowledge may make it superficial. For travelers by air, great cities may soon become only stopping-places on a world journey; and that too may make men superficial.

A second bad effect of the new travel-machines is sometimes thought to be important. It is often said that modern life is more of a *rush* and a *noise* than life used to be; and even leisure is said to be nowadays only a confused hurrying from one thing to another. This is said to be caused largely by the motor-car; and so this charge may have to be added to the charge of superficiality. But it is difficult to decide whether in fact many are hurt by the rush and hurry. So many seem to be still "going slow" in their minds that perhaps we have not yet reached the point of overstrain. It is true that some feel the "fret" and pressure of modern streets full of cars; but exactly the same complaint was made about the rush and hurry of stage-coaches when, as Mr. Drinkwater says in his Memoirs, the coach from Edinburgh to London covered the distance of 400 miles in 40 hours. Perhaps the pressure and labor of earlier forms of travel was greater than ours.

But even so, there may be some restlessness which is due to the fact that the motor-car affects some minds unduly.

What then are we to say of the general effects on our civilization of the new travel-machines? Anthropologists give us accounts of the effects which follow when European inventions are introduced among Africans or Polynesians. There is an account in George Calderon's essays of a deacon of a church in Polynesia who, being Europeanized, attended service in a starched evening shirt and nothing else. Such misunderstandings and misuses of new opportunities are always possible. We in this generation are like savages to whom for the first time the motor-car and the aëroplane have been introduced; and it is not unlikely therefore that we are unskilful in the use of our new tools.

We are not concerned here with politics, still less with international affairs; but it cannot be forgotten that the internal-combustion engine, in the motor and the aëroplane and submarine, has been used to increase the destructiveness of war and to make war more likely by increasing the fear of each nation for its neighbors' "tanks" and bombing air-craft. Some of those in power in public affairs have not yet grasped the fact that common folk in all countries do not want "prestige" or "national glory," but only bread and clothes and quiet enjoyment; and these noble savages who rule us have suddenly been presented, by a science they do not understand, with new instruments. These instruments therefore they turn to ancient savage uses. Instead of increasing the safety of aëroplanes, money and brains are spent in making them more useful for throwing bombs. Instead of developing motor traffic across all frontiers, each government is mechanizing its armies; so that tanks and tractors for big guns may terrify its neighbors more effectually. The insecurity and fear, which have been increased in the world by the aëroplane and the motor, are much worse effects than any superficiality of mind of which they may be the causes. But this evil and barbarous use of new inventions ought not to be taken as an argument against those inventions. If our contemporary savages had not misused their opportunities, we should not still expect war—we should have organized peace on a new and securer basis. But this example may show how little the new instruments are themselves to blame. Savages may be unprepared to use wisely what is new to them. In any case, let us look again at the uses of motor-cars outside of working hours. The anthropologist in England or America should be able to see how, with greater skill, the new instruments may improve instead of degrading our civilization. And in fact *not* every one is being made superficial by motor-cars. An increasing number of people are becoming, as all should be, more civilized in the new sense. First, the continual and close contact with many different people has been shown above to be changing the basis of manners from that which is characteristic of a "caste" society, where the manners of the rich are of one kind and those of the manual worker of another, that of shops and streets different from that of drawing-rooms; and as a result, the manners in streets and shops are not only more democratic but also much better than they were fifty years ago. There is more "consideration" for the seller on the part of the buyer; and in the streets more friendliness of each passer-by for every other. But this improvement of manners in common life is due in part to the new mixing of people in the new transport system.

Secondly, the attitude of *travelers* toward life and the world is spreading in wider circles. Men are less "stuck" in their minds than they were even thirty years ago. We feel that modern civilization is not a fixed point to be reached, but a process of which our own daily lives form parts. We are going on. Where we came from and where we are now, are less interesting than where we are going to; and at least among the young, it is *not* terrifying to be told that the economic and political system to which we are accustomed is passing away. To some indeed it is a positive relief to feel that Parliament is "done for," and also the city and the church and the gold standard. But perhaps this suggestion would terrify others. It may not be true that any of these old works of art *is* obsolete. But the feeling that they are obsolete—whether correct or not—has no terrors for those who are moving on. The sailor regrets to hear that the port he left has been destroyed by an earthquake; but he is bound for another port. The modern mind is on the road and on the pathless air; and this uprooting of the mind has been in part the effect of motor-cars.

The mind has become nomadic again. As General Smuts said at the end of the war— "Humanity has struck its tents and is on the move," or as the contrast used at the beginning of this chapter implied, we are having experience of a change from the outlook of the agriculturist to that of the sailor. This does not imply any disdain of the past. There are periods in which the minds of men take root and grow into an established system; and all that is desired by reformers in such periods is that men shall live up to the ideals they have inherited. There are other periods, such as the Renaissance in Europe, when men's minds are on the move. That is our experience now. Our chief task is not to live up to the old ideals: it is to find new ideals worth living up to.

V

MOVING PICTURES AND RADIO

INTO the world already changed by the new customs and attitudes so far discussed, the new machines for entertainment—the phonograph, the moving pictures and the radio, have introduced even more radical changes.[1] The use of leisure has obviously been transformed for millions of people in all countries by these new mechanisms. Their effects upon men's minds differ greatly in different backgrounds; and, no doubt, their most disturbing effects occur in Asia and Africa, where the phonograph, the moving picture, and the radio operate in a primitive or medieval background of magic and traditionalism. But these mechanisms belong to our tradition; they are merely a few among many mechanisms which are the natural outcome of a century of the applications of science; and they are expressions of the same ability to remodel tradition which is to be seen in the productive processes

---

[1] The best recent summary of the serious discussion of the movies is "The Film in National Life," Report of a Commission (Allen and Unwin, London, June, 1932).

and the normal life of Western civilization. They are not alien mysteries; and therefore their effects in our civilization must be estimated by reference to other changes which are occurring while they are being introduced. For us, who are not Asiatic, nor African, the phonograph, moving picture, and radio operate in a community already educated enough to read, a city population highly industrialized. Secondly, it should be noted that many of the effects of these mechanisms are much more transitory and trivial than social observers are inclined to suppose; because most of those who go to the movies or use the radio do so merely for a momentary relief. And thirdly, it should be remembered that the new mechanisms for entertainment depend for their existence upon large numbers of people with small incomes. They are not luxuries of the few; they are already commonplaces for the many. That is the most important fact about them. They are examples of the same process as that which produced cheap clothing in the nineteenth century and cheap tea. The application of machine production to the provision of entertainment has made the kind of entertainment hitherto available only for a few and only occasionally, now available for many and available every day.

I shall not attempt to discuss all the effects of

this new situation, nor even the majority of these effects; because I want to concentrate attention upon one fundamental social effect of machines for entertainment which seems to me to be most significant for the future. It is this. The new machines for entertainment make for similarity of outlook and attitude among people of very different occupations, incomes, or social classes and, in a smaller degree, for similarity of outlook and attitude among different nations. The phonograph, moving picture, and radio are bridging the traditional gaps between distinct groups of people. They produce in leisure the same sort of effect that similar clothing produces, both at work and in leisure. This does not imply that they are making those who belong to different social classes more friendly, nor that they are making nations more peaceful. The more you know of other people, the more you may dislike them. Bridging the gap may be only increasing the tendency to fight on the bridge. But nowadays those who belong to any one social or national group have more similar ideas and a more similar attitude to that prevailing in other groups than they had fifty years ago.

This new similarity of outlook and attitude is important for two reasons—first, because the new mechanisms give much greater power for affecting great masses of men in the same way, if any group in control wishes to use such power; and secondly because they promote an unconscious growth of new attitudes where no deliberate policy guides the use of moving picture and radio. Consider, first, the deliberate use of the new instruments. The Soviet government, for example, makes carefully considered use of the movies and the radio. The Five Year Plan is explained in film pictures; and enthusiasm for the work involved in the Plan is aroused by showing on the screen what has been done and what can be done. Similarly the radio is used by the Soviet government to persuade or to incite its subjects to coöperation in the Plan. All governments tend to use the radio for obtaining that general support which cannot be so quickly, nor so safely, aroused through newspapers or platform speeches.[2] If war occurs, the moving picture and the radio will certainly make the peoples at war more amenable to the policy of their governments. The radio, we must remember, had not yet become so easily available for influencing the people in the World War, but there are disastrous pos-

[2] Controversies arise out of the use of the radio by governments which are not by profession dictatorships. Thus the German government used the radio in the presidential election of 1932 to oppose the candidature of Hitler, and there was an attempt later on by his supporters to raise legal objections to this use. In Great Britain, the "National" government overbalanced its case against the Labor Party by the use of the radio in the election of 1931.

MOVING PICTURES AND RADIO

sibilities for its use in creating hate or fear in future wars.

The new mechanisms involve a much greater centralization of power in the hands of a few in every country; and whatever may be said of this new concentration of power in the hands of those who control governments, it is useful to note the difference that the movies and radio have made in politics and in industrial organization. In the first place, the *rate* of social change can be very much increased. The slow methods of popular discussion from which our parliamentary system arose, were somewhat improved by the press. But even the press operates less quickly than the moving picture and radio, in modifying the outlook and forming the opinions of great masses of people. An example is given in the B.B.C. Yearbook for 1931, where the purchase of Saving Certificates is shown to have been speeded up by a radio speech from Sir Josiah Stamp. It is now possible, by skilful use of the new machinery for what is called "propaganda," to induce quickly a general modification of age-long beliefs and customs. Habits, indeed, are still slow in their growth and insecure until they have been, as it were, embedded in daily life for some years; but we must not imagine that because it took nearly a century to industrialize England, it will therefore take a century to industrialize Russia or China or even parts of Africa. Even in countries already industrialized much quicker social changes may occur than have occurred hitherto. *The instruments of social change are more efficient than ever before.* Here then, in the films and the radio, we have the most valuable and most dangerous instruments of education. They are dangerous because they require for the success of their use in changing society a very great centralization of control. They are forms of education very suitable to dictatorship; and every man knows how excellent a dictatorship would be—if he were the dictator! In any case, if the central control is good, the effect of its influence is good. If otherwise—then otherwise!

Whatever, then, in any country may be the present use of movie and radio, owing to the power they give in assimilating the opinions of great numbers, they mark the beginnings of a new civilization in which the rate of change can be quicker. The "unreality" of much political controversy is generally recognized; but a good instance of "unreality" was to be found in the recent very transitory discussion in Great Britain of the referendum as a method of discovering public opinion. Clearly whether a referendum is good or bad, the means for using it have been greatly improved by the radio. But no one, in the political dispute, even referred to the new possibilities of radio in asking a question and in discovering what people thought. Similarly we hear something of diplomacy and international friction; but very seldom is any one aware of the opportunities now available, thróugh moving pictures and radio, of presenting to any nation the case of another nation or the character of the issues involved. Indeed we do not seem to be yet aware of the great social uses to which these inventions could be put. "Representation" by elected members of assemblies will change its character, if the "represented"—the citizens, can be consulted at once and directly. Changes of law and administration can be more speedily agreed and made operative, if we depend less upon print than upon sight of persons and speech. Different opinions on public affairs can be heard on the radio by the great majority who do not attend meetings; and those who have no desire to be elected as "representatives"—poets or essayists, for example—can discuss public issues from a non-political point of view, on the radio.

The sound-film also has changed political technique. Thousands can now see and hear those who are in control of public policy. They could follow

—if the "news films" were more intelligently made, the more important events abroad—not sporting items, nor military reviews, but the unloading of ships in great ports or the gathering of the raw material for industry. This use of the moving picture is beginning in certain schools, in the teaching of history and geography; and some schools are making their own films. But we have hardly begun to use the social power which movie and radio provide, although a revolution in the instruments of social change has occurred which may prove to be as important as the introduction of printing. We are like people who have electrical power available and do not use it. A well-designed social change could be made in less than a generation, if we chose deliberately to use film and radio as they might be used.

Let us turn now to the second kind of assimilation of ideas and outlook—the undesigned effect of movie and radio. In most countries, outside Russia, the moving picture is not controlled by any one group in power. There is no deliberate policy expressed in the films shown.[3] And the radio also in most countries is uncontrolled by any one group. There is therefore no single deliberate policy ex-

---

[3] For the Censorship of Films in various countries, see two articles in the Manchester Guardian, May 9 and 10, 1932.

MOVING PICTURES AND RADIO 83

pressed in the greater part of the world through the new mechanisms. But the assimilation of outlook and attitude among different social classes occurs none the less; and the general character of that assimilation can be described. We may consider, then, what the films and radio are doing, without deliberate policy, in making people think and feel in the same way.

It will be easier to discuss the situation if the movie or talkie is taken first. It is suitable only for the entertainment of great numbers. Several million people must see a film before it becomes a "paying proposition"; and the sort of entertainment provided, is what those in control think is already desired by great numbers. No change of taste is intended to occur as a result of seeing films; but obviously, if one kind of taste is satisfied, that kind becomes more dominant or fixed over larger sections of society. Thus a more general similarity in outlook and attitude seems to be growing up, because most of the time at the pictures each of us has to look at what others enjoy, in order to enjoy occasionally what we ourselves enjoy best. The result is the almost unconscious formation of certain general ideas. For example, if a great number of film stories show Chicago as a place in which gangsters are usually shooting in the streets, a general feeling arises that it is dangerous to live in Chicago. Now I lived four months in Chicago in 1929; and I never saw a gangster's quarrel, never heard a shot fired. I heard some admirable music and saw some good paintings; and I discussed with many able and very public-spirited men and women the rehousing in the negro quarter which had actually been done and the educational experiments which provide examples for the whole world. But when I speak to any one in England about Chicago, I find that they know nothing about it except stories of gangsters. Similarly, an investigation of the opinions of school-children in Wales has shown that many of them believe the Chinese to be murderous villains, because of what they have seen on the films. The undesigned result of many films is to fix in a great number of minds quite fantastic and seriously mistaken ideas about foreign peoples. This is exercising the thought of those in control of government in Asiatic countries and in Africa; for the opinion of Europeans that is being established in those countries, through films, may undermine all European influence. And even among the European peoples themselves, the moving picture in Great Britain, for example, is establishing strange ideas of what happens in France or Germany or America. But, clearly, some of the fixed ideas derived from films are by no means bad; and such ideas might be excellent, if the attitude of the producers were more intelligent. Even as things now stand, it is good that people have some idea how other people live; and this they could not so easily have acquired without the movies. It is obvious that any government in control of moving pictures could concentrate hatred or hostility upon any of its opponents, at home or abroad; but the unconscious growth of fixed opinions which is the unintended result of film stories, is more important. These fixed opinions have reference not only to foreign peoples, but also to other social classes than one's own or to people in occupations not one's own. On the whole, the film-story makers cannot afford to indulge in national or social hatred or suspicion; for hatred and suspicion are not good entertainment. People on the films are presented as if they were more interesting than dangerous, even if they are crooks or villains. Even in Java, India, and China, the peculiar habits of Hollywood are much more likely to make the Asiatic spectator laugh than to make him anti-European. Asiatic peoples are not such fools as to imagine that everybody in Europe behaves as the funny people on the films do; for indeed they have their own stories in the East, which are both plain-spoken and sufficiently scandalous.

Unfortunately most of those who criticize the effect of films upon other people do not seem to have seen many films. They are generally "superior" persons. But only those who do not enjoy stories or gossip suppose that such enjoyment must be corrupting. The most virtuous of all my friends read "crook" stories; but I do not find that I have to watch the spoons when they come to see me. Therefore I refuse to believe that ordinary folk are corrupted by entertaining stories about villains.[4]

On the whole the film story has widened the minds of our generation and added considerably to the interests of the majority. We are in general more aware of social customs different from ours, either because those who are represented on the films belong to different social groupings than our own or because they belong to other nations. Exactly the same stories are being put before people in all classes, in most of the big towns of any one country; and these same stories are being followed on the screen in Russia and Asia, not to speak of France and Germany. Languages divide men; but a comic situation or a beautiful face looks the same in all classes and in all nations. Moving pictures

---

[4] The Home Secretary (Sir H. Samuel) in a speech in the House of Commons (April 15, 1932) said that "his very expert and experienced advisers in the Home Office were of opinion that, on the whole, the cinema conduced more to the prevention of crime than to its commission."

make it possible for people with very different amounts of income to see the same stage-plays; but there are no theaters using actors at which one can find entertainment at any time of an afternoon or evening for the comparatively small amount charged at many movie houses. In the movies the entertainment is of the same kind for the poorer and the richer quarters of a city, for the market-town of an agricultural area and for the industrial city or the mining district.

The similarity of outlook and attitude due to the films is shown not only by common views of nations or members of any one social class, but also by common admirations for film stars. The names, features, and habits of a few "stars" are known in all social classes and in many different nations. Societies exist for the enduring worship of Rudolph Valentino after his death, and of Greta Garbo. Indeed, the statesmen of the world are not half so well known as film stars—partly perhaps because these stars work harder at what is called "publicity." Again, there are much more generally accepted manners and customs with regard to what is called "love" because of the films. In Japan, the censorship does not allow a kiss to continue for more than fifteen feet of film; but American embraces are more lengthy, and they have their effect upon the habits of the younger generation. All over the world, however, the same conventions are being introduced by film stars; and we have only to watch the younger generation of youths and girls as they walk in the streets to see the effect of the movies. Watch how they treat one another—and how much more skilful they are than the village yokel following traditional methods. Finally, the movies fill many minds with the same figures, stories, incidents, and ideas. The mental world for great numbers of children as well as adults is fuller than it used to be and also more similar because of this method of entertainment. And this change has occurred just at a time when, first, more work in industry is repetition work and, secondly, there is a much greater amount of uncertainty about the future. Those who do repetition work in industry tend to day-dreaming. Their minds are free from guiding the actual movement of their hands, and can therefore play upon all kinds of ideas; but the films provide many of these ideas and so fill up what might otherwise be empty spaces. As for uncertainty, new ideas are put into people's heads as to the dress they ought to wear and the manners they ought to have. In a time of flexible or changing custom, therefore, these pictures on the screen tend both to unsettle established habits and to incite to new habits; and they do so for great numbers in many different social classes and many different nations, at the same time.

The use of leisure for going to the movies has made some difference also to the relation between the sexes; for it has become the habit of men and women and especially of young men and young women to find their entertainment together at "the pictures." This may tend toward equality of status for women as well as toward a greater assimilation of the points of view of women and men with regard to personal relationships. The most obvious contrast with what occurred fifty years ago is to be seen if one compares the companionship at the pictures with the custom of that earlier time when the men congregated in public-houses or saloons and the women enjoyed gossip on doorsteps. Even among the few with larger incomes and more "elegant" traditions, it was the custom for the sexes to be more separate in their leisure than they now are.

With this use of the movies for companionship and common interest may be connected the prevalence of love stories on the films and the advertising of what is crudely called "sex attraction." The moving picture is blamed by some critics for promoting eroticism. But it is to be feared that such critics do not know how much sexual interest exists normally and did exist long before projectors were invented. Indeed the popularity of subjects with a "sex" interest on the films is partly a revolt against the repression in the traditional morality. That is too large an issue to be discussed here; but it must not be assumed that the younger generation who now find pleasure in love episodes on the screen are worse than their forefathers who, at least in the towns, used to attend at the music-halls and gin-palaces of an earlier time. If the interest in sexual attraction to-day is franker, it is considerably less coarse than it used to be. And if, as is indeed probable, there is far too much attention paid by the films to the more trivial aspects of the relation between the sexes, that may provide a sort of sublimation of passion for the many workers who are in fact sexually starved, not so much with regard to the cruder expression of the sex impulses as with regard to those many slight and seemingly trivial satisfactions which a civilized society provides in easy converse between persons of opposite sex. What is unhealthy in the "sex appeal" of films is due to a disease or repression or complex in contemporary society quite independent of the screen: and the films so far from increasing may even relieve the strain.

Moving pictures may also be providing some satisfaction in beauty of form and grace or delicacy of surroundings. A pretty face and a finely shaped body are not to be found in every street; and perhaps without the films many would be unaware how powerful such things may be. Common folk may discover on the screen some of the truths known to the Greeks; for, as it will be argued later, in some uses of modern leisure, we are restoring "the body" to its rightful throne. But many of the criticisms of film pictures come from those who are blind to bodily beauty or, being themselves abnormally repressed, overestimate the disturbance which the perception of beautiful forms may cause in common folk.

As for the social effects of the radio, perhaps the most general is the increase of entertainment at home. This may have the effect of keeping people nearer to the rest of their families; but it would be an exaggeration to say that it brought them more closely into touch with their homes. Indeed, entertainment at home by radio really involves another invasion of the narrow world of home by a wider world outside. Owing to the radio there is more, not less, common feeling and common attitude in a whole community. The community formed by frequent listeners is more easily moved by the same opinions and affected by the same tastes. The poorer quarters and poorer homes are listening to the same entertainment as the richer. The doctor and the dustman laugh at the same jokes at the same time. Vaudeville and music seem to be the most important parts of the radio programs, so far as the effect upon the majority of listeners goes; and these again are the same at the same time for those in different social classes, different environments and even different nations. We have, therefore, since the coming of radio, in about 1925, into a great number of homes, a more light-hearted community and possibly one with a more general appreciation of music. Apart from the social effects of deliberate policy on the radio, popular tendencies are strengthened without being noticeably changed in character. On the other hand, radio has filled with entertainment of one sort or another many hours of the new leisure, which, without radio, would have been perhaps unendurable. Thus radio has reinforced the common attitude toward leisure in making it seem more valuable; and therefore it may be more difficult than it was in earlier times to lengthen hours of work or to decrease the opportunities for using leisure. The general "set" of the mind of great numbers is toward a fuller appreciation of the uses of leisure.

The most important recent social change however is the tendency to set a high value upon assimilation of ideas through the moving picture and the radio. This assimilation supports an assumption of social equality, because when those who are of very different occupations and incomes see the same films and listen to the same radio entertainments, the part of the world of thought or imagination which is common to all social classes is increased. Each assumes that others know what he means and in this sense at least, each tends to treat the other as an equal. Therefore manners tend to be more similar in all classes; and clothes and houses and even tones of speech follow the same pattern. The tradition of social snobbery in Great Britain seems to resist all modern tendencies to equality; and therefore perhaps new ways of distinguishing himself or herself from the vulgar herd are being developed by the clerk or the school-teacher or the skilled engineer. But on the whole the movie and the radio are making the members of most modern communities assume that those whom they meet are similar in outlook and manners. They are undermining the consciousness of class distinctions.

Such a tendency toward equality may not be good if the level at which we are assimilated is not high. In other words, that society is desirable in which the garbage-man and the grocer and the bus-conductor have the same sort of tastes and the same background of opinion as the scholar or the lawyer; but only if these same tastes include a taste for music and the background of opinion is one of reliance upon exact knowledge and hostility to traditional superstitions. I do not underestimate the value of other tastes—such as the taste for tobacco and beer, which have their place, nor do I repudiate all superstition, because nobody is without some superstition. In any case, the sense of equality is promoted by common sights and sounds, through the moving picture and radio; and if we compare popular tastes in entertainment to-day with those of fifty years ago, it will be found that the new tastes are on a higher level.

Whether they are higher or lower, however, is less important for our present argument than that they are similar for thousands in all classes and in many nations. The common basis of general ideas and generally understood customs over great areas of social life, creates a situation which has never hitherto occurred. Social equality and mutual understanding across the boundaries of nations have long been preached as ideals; but perhaps the form in which both are being realized is so entirely unexpected that the new situation is not recognized for what it is. The current of any social impulse can now run through a whole nation and across the boundaries of nations much more freely than ever before. This may not necessarily be good; for evil impulses may spread as fast as others. But the whole situation in the relationship between human beings is much more fluid, more plastic, more unstable: and the forces at work are not all of them the deliberate influences of those with a gospel—whether traditional or revolutionary; for undesigned and unconsidered effects follow upon the new uses of leisure, when men, women, and children are seeking only entertainment.

VI

WAYS OF ESCAPE

THE increase in the amount of leisure and in the opportunities for using it have brought into prominence the value of leisure as a means of escaping from the defects of everyday life. Nobody's work is without some sort of disagreeable elements. Indeed the mere fact that it has to be done at regular hours annoys some people. And even the rest of life, outside of working hours, is not generally so enjoyable that one can accept any entertainment that offers without feeling discontent at its inadequacy. It is good to escape from ourselves occasionally, not to speak of our friends and acquaintances; and leisure is the time for escape. We seek relief, even for a few moments, from what we may call "real" life—or, at any rate, our usual life.

From this point of view the movies and the radio provide ways of escape from ordinary life into a new common world of thought or imagination. But that is evidently not enough for some of us. Among the other "ways of escape" which are common nowadays, which have developed in the recent past, two of the most significant are gambling and hiking—or other forms of going into the country. These two modern ways of escape may be taken as typical of two contradictory tendencies in the modern uses of leisure. They represent two very different desires, two very different kinds of enjoyment. Some like one way of escape; others like another; and in our civilization one kind of person often does not know what the other kind is doing. The opportunities for using leisure in the modern world are various; and people's tastes differ. But that is not the whole story. Different opportunities for using leisure are provided by different sorts of organization, and some of these organizations are deliberately established for purposes which are directly opposed to the purposes promoted by other organizations. Gambling provides a way of escape from monotony by excitement; and country rambles provide a way of escape from monotony by quiet. Excitement and quiet are the very different enjoyments desired by different people or perhaps by the same people at different times. Let us see how they are obtained to-day.

Gambling of one sort or another is, obviously, common in all countries and as old as human history. In China it has been, for about a thousand years, one of the chief obstacles to progress. In the eighteenth century in Europe gambling at cards absorbed much of the energies of the richer classes; and this form of gambling still survives. But the form of gambling which has developed greatly within the past thirty years in Great Britain is betting on sporting events. One of the effects of this excitement about the results of "sports" or "games" is the massing of spectators at a few horse-races and at many football matches. The new transport system has made it possible for increasing numbers to go to the Derby, for example. Similarly football matches "draw" increasing numbers of spectators every year. There are traditional "events," the popularity of which is increased by the press and more recently by the radio and also by the advertisements of the transit companies which make money out of crowds. Being a spectator in a very large crowd is a modern and, in fact, very recent experience, which may be enjoyable in itself. But the important new social fact, for our present purpose, is the losing or winning of money in connection with these events. The chief purpose of the new betting is to obtain excitement, but there is also the hope of money gain, which seems to survive all disappointment. An elaborate and very expensive organization is maintained for the provision of a sufficient number of sporting events to keep the excitement going. The newspapers assist in giving opportunities to everybody for excitement every day and at most hours of the day; and indeed the whole social system connected with sporting events would make a very good subject for investigation by an anthropologist familiar with the more primitive forms of custom.

Betting on British "sporting events" has very greatly increased since 1900, and chiefly since the war. Also, it has increased mainly among women; and betting by children is now commoner than it ever was, if indeed it occurred at all before 1900—which is doubtful. But it is impossible here to describe the new methods.[1]

More than four million people in Great Britain are betting regularly; and, in some factories and workshops, nine out of every ten men employed have that habit. In 1910 the amount staked on horse-racing was about fifty-two million pounds; and on football about forty-eight millions. But nowadays the amount staked every year on horse-racing alone is about two hundred million pounds; and in addition, from fifty to a hundred millions

[1] The best published information is in the evidence given before the Select Committee on the Betting Duty in 1923; and there is a small book called "Betting Facts" by E. Benson Perkins, which gives a summary of this evidence.

are staked on football and other events. The number of bookmakers and their agents is over fifty thousand. There is no doubt at all that this form of excitement is more highly organized than it was in 1900. The law which prevents some forms of betting, the Betting Act of 1853, was passed, as the date indicates, before the days of the telegraph and the telephone. Even before the war the Post Office services had greatly assisted the increase of betting; and now about seven per cent of ordinary telegrams and ten per cent of press telegrams deal with horse-races. Thus through the Post Office services, the state supports the tendency to increase the amount of betting. Also greyhound racing has been introduced in order to increase the opportunities for small bets; and the organization for the supply of betting news has been very much improved.

The most rapid increase of betting has occurred since the World War. This is due to several very different causes. The excitement of wartime became almost habitual, and the desire for excitement has continued since the war. Luck seemed during wartime to have a large part to play in the fortunes of both men and women; and the worship of the Goddess Luck is very attractive. Women had larger amounts of money during the war and immediately after; and besides, the growth of unemployment and the uncertainty of millions, from week to week, as to their future increased the desire to risk something for a possible gain. The more insecure a man or woman feels, the more reckless he or she is, in the risks taken.

Finally, the system for collecting bets has been very much more highly organized. Men and sometimes women go round from house to house in some quarters to collect bets. Even in some schools there are secret arrangements for collecting bets from children. In some towns small shopkeepers take the bets of the neighborhood; in others newspaper sellers at street corners collect bets; and some unemployed men and women have managed to live by acting as touts or runners for bookmakers. Upon all this is built the office and race-course organization of the powerful and wealthy bookmakers who call themselves Turf Commission Agents and advertise in the newspapers.

The organization of betting might make an economist doubtful whether the demand created the supply or the supply the demand. Undoubtedly great numbers of women would not bet if the opportunities for betting were not so many and so easily available. On the other hand, the desire to bet is certainly strong enough and common enough to support large numbers of bookmakers, even if they made no effort to increase their business. The fundamental fact is that men and women in modern life want excitement. Their daily lives are dull. Their prospects are, if not gloomy, at any rate not entrancing. Most of them are living in such a way that the addition of a little more money would mean at least a momentary escape from care; and quite apart from the hope of gain, which must, after a few experiences, have become dim even among the most optimistic of those who bet, there is always pleasure in anticipation before the results are known. Indeed probably more pleasure is derived from "counting chickens before they are hatched" than in seeing the chickens when they do happen to be hatched; certainly more pleasure is gained in anticipation than is lost in disappointment. The pleasure lasts for some days; but the disappointment is momentary and easily forgotten. Also the fact that many people are excited at the same time about the same event increases the pleasurable excitement of each.

Money spent in obtaining pleasurable excitement is not "lost," as money paid for seats at a theater is not lost. The excitement due to horse-race results or football results probably interferes with work in some factories and distracts some women from household occupations; but occupations are not always more valuable than the relief one can secure from them. Sporting events and probably also gambling provide material for many conversations. At the high table of a Cambridge College I have joined in a general conversation about the probable results in the coming Grand National, although I knew nothing about it and I suspect none of the others in the conversation did either. But it is easy to make conversation by telling a person what that same person told you five minutes before; and the conversation of most "sportsmen" is on that level.

On the other hand, the use of leisure for excitement about possible money gains is civilization at a very low level, if it is civilization at all. The same form of excitement makes crowds cheer a declaration of war or lap up the details of a murder. The appetite for money gain is corroding to leisure and imparts to it the atmosphere of the jungle; but we are so unskilful socially that we miss half the opportunities for civilizing leisure, and crude outlets are sought for desires which might equally well be satisfied by other and less crude methods. The chief social effect over a whole community of the existing method of obtaining relief from monotony through excitement is the formation of large groups of men and women who are unstable in mind, superstitious, reckless, and absorbed in the appetite for money gain. Such groups have to be reckoned with, in considering public affairs—the future of peace or war, of reaction or reform. No more need be said. But the social effects of the particular methods of getting excitement to-day must not lead to a condemnation of all excitement. Excitement could be provided otherwise than by gambling; and in any case, betting is better than head-hunting or gladiatorial combats or the public torture of criminals or street violence—the earlier methods of escaping from everyday life by excitement.

Now let us turn to the very different tendency of some people, and happily young people, to seek a way of escape in the quiet that still survives outside the city streets. I have watched large groups of these young men and women, in walking clothes, going out on the street-cars from Vienna to the hills near by, on a Sunday morning. I have seen similar groups going out in running shorts from Hamburg. I have met such groups on the roads in the country in America, and in the outskirts of London and Glasgow and Manchester. I do not want to idealize the movement of which such groups are the outcome; but it is clearly a sort of escape from the conditions under which life in a city area is carried on; and the escape is made into the countryside. Now the country-side, for people in industrial areas, is as close as they can get to what we call "Nature." It is not the sort of Nature which is to be found in deserts or oceans, on untrodden hills or in trackless forests; but it is the best sort of Nature available for the majority in modern cities. Even a country road is more open to light and air and is quieter than a city street. Space and wider skies are to be found outside the city area; and the younger generation—perhaps because of the new education—is beginning to value such things. The escape they desire is not found in the excitement of gambling but in the enjoyment of their own energies and in quiet.

No doubt some of the young men and women who form the new movement find excitement also in companionship or in the adventure of visits to new places. But such excitement is obviously very different in character from the excitement sought in gambling. It is the more civilized excitement to be found in the hitherto unexplored use of one's own abilities; and this can be combined with a delight in aloofness from the commonplace, which is the enjoyment of quiet. Indeed it is significant that, while modern inventions have provided for more and more entertainment and thus increased the dependence of great numbers upon professional entertainers, some of the younger generation find in hiking or rambling a method of enjoyment which does not depend upon being entertained. A certain self-sufficiency in leisure was recognized, among ancient philosophers, as the condition for the most fruitful enjoyment of leisure. But the capacity for enjoying "one's self," in the narrowest sense of that phrase, as contrasted with the ability to be entertained by others, requires skill for its highest development. Very few know what resources are within themselves; but the movement of the youth toward hiking and rambling may be a means for discovering unsuspected abilities of intelligence and emotion.

The history of this new movement is interesting. Its full development is most obvious in Germany, where "Youth Hostels" for walkers were established as far back as 1909. At first the school buildings, which stood empty during the summer holidays, were used as shelters for the night for those who went on walking tours: and now there is an association with 130,000 individual members, besides corporate members—12,000 schools and 13,500 clubs. There are now about 2,200 youth hostels in Germany; and in 1930 over four million, mostly under twenty-one years of age, spent a night in them. In England, Scotland, and Wales also the same movement is growing; and the British Youth Hostels Association already has about eighty hostels in various parts of England and Wales for the use of walkers and cyclists. The Scottish Youth Hostels Association provides similar services in Scotland. The charge for the night is kept low, generally about one shilling; and the hostels are used by increasing numbers of those under twenty-five years of age. But this is only one step in a movement which was represented in the Camping Club, since 1901, and the Federation of Rambling Clubs since 1905. The Youth Hostels Association was founded in 1930.

The social importance of all such movements or groups is in the contrast between what they stand for and what is represented by the desire for excitement in gambling. The country walkers and cyclists are finding their enjoyment in their own activities, not in looking on, nor in waiting for some one else to win a victory in some sporting contest. They are finding some of their enjoyment in companionship; and it is important that girls and young men are going out together, for this sharing of the same enjoyment by girls and young men is not possible in most games. It has a civilizing effect upon manners and customs, far more important than the traditionally overestimated effect upon character of contests in games and sports.

Above all, the return to the country is important

in so far as it represents an asceticism of enjoyment, because it aims at an escape, not into excitement, but into quiet—not merely quiet from external noises but also quiet of mind, which is freedom from care. The use of leisure for escape into that kind of quiet is one of the most necessary elements in the complex of activities which we call civilized life; for quiet of mind is one of the sources of poetry and the other arts.

Such quiet is ascetic because it is the result of a conscious restriction of many of one's capacities, in order that a finer enjoyment may be derived from the simplest tastes; for just as a painter in the Chinese tradition may obtain his most valuable results by the use of the simplest means, so in the art of life one may reject obvious means of enjoyment in order to use more skilfully one's ability to enjoy a very little. The enjoyment of quiet implies an independence of everything but the current of one's own mind in its contact with the world of nature. In quiet of mind "the world" is well lost.

But there is another contrast between the passion for excitement and the desire for quiet, which relates to the "economic" aspect of these two tendencies. The cost to the individual of the excitement derived from betting, is rather large. The proportion of money spent on gambling by the comparatively poor, in their appetite for excitement, is very large as compared with the amount spent on their food and clothing. But clearly there are more inducements in the modern world to spend on betting, than there used to be thirty years ago. By contrast, it is not expensive to gratify the desire for quiet. Those who enjoy sitting in the sun or walking in the country-side, do not spend so much money upon their pleasures; and indeed it seemed to me that in Vienna and Hamburg, where I was staying when an economic crisis had greatly increased poverty, hundreds of the younger generation were learning to enjoy what did not cost much money. Money is only a sign of one's power over other men; and money spent in leisure makes one's enjoyment depend upon other men's services. But some can enjoy themselves without having entertainment provided; and that is being discovered by the younger generation who go for "rambles" in the country-side. Here again, but now in an economic sense, is asceticism in the use of leisure.

A new civilization is revealed by the two important characteristics in the ways of escape which have recently become most popular. One characteristic is the desire for excitement, the other is the desire for calm and quiet. Perhaps the same people sometimes want excitement and at other times want quiet;

but it seems more probable that two different kinds of people are using modern opportunities in leisure. It would be foolish to suppose that one kind of person was "better" than the other or "superior" to the other; for we know too little about human beings to condemn natural reactions without studying them much more closely. Those who want excitement, as well as those who want quiet, may be only searching for compensations for what they lack in the rest of their lives. For example, excitement may be wanted in leisure because most of working life is dull; and the duller it is, the cruder the excitement which is satisfying. Perhaps the excitement of head-hunting among some savages was due to the monotony of the greater part of their lives. Now we don't go head-hunting, except when relief from the monotony of peace is sought in war. Generally we go to races or football matches, and bet in order to get more excitement out of them.

It is more difficult to see what is implied in the new development of walks in the country-side. Clearly there has always been a certain discomfort in city streets; and those who have been able, have escaped. But now increasing numbers, especially of young people, manage to escape from the streets in which their lives are spent. Some, who make a parade of being "hikers," shout and make wild noises in their journeys, apparently in order to show that they are on holiday. The same sort of shouting occurs on Hampstead Heath on bank holidays; but it is only a violent explosion after too much repression. In the same way the cruder type of "tripper" leaves torn paper and other rubbish where he has been on holiday. But why blame the way in which he takes a holiday? That is crude, because his normal life is crude. What is happening in these cases is the spilling of the slum into the countryside; but the people who are compelled to live in noisy factories and overcrowded houses have no choice in their occupations or their houses; and their manners and customs are formed by conditions for which they have no responsibility. The fact that some of them lose their heads—and their manners—when they go outside the city streets, is as much resented by others who come from city streets for quiet as it can be by those who live in happier circumstances. It is ridiculous, however, to suppose that the majority of those who go hiking are barbarians. Their return to the country-side is indeed a sign of civilization; for most of them are seeking an escape from city noise and hurry.

The social effect of this tendency may be less widespread but it is by no means less important than the social effect of gambling. In the first place, because the leisure of workers is generally longest on Sundays, the new custom of hiking and rambling has decreased the attendance at church services among the younger generation. A Committee of the Church of England reports . . . "another cause of the decline in Sunday School attendances and of the difficulty of getting adequate supplies of teachers, is the change in the habits and outlook of people, which has come about in recent years, largely since and probably also largely as a result of the war. There has been a general revolt against what may be termed the older 'Sabbatarian' view of the Lord's Day. . . . The movement for Sunday amusements has had widespread success." [2] Those who desire to maintain the Sabbatarian view are evidently unable to see what is happening as anything more than a desire for what they call "amusements." But those who go into the country-side certainly do not lack admiration for the beauty or sublimity of Nature: and those who regret the exodus should consult St. Bernard's letter to the founder of Fountains Abbey, when he left the city of York for what was then the wilderness: "You will find among woods and rocks what you cannot learn from human teachers." The desertion of

[2] Report of the Bishop of Southwark's Commission, 1931.

the churches does not indicate that religion is decaying, although its form may be changing.

The general effect throughout any city community of a closer contact with quiet outside the city may turn out to be fundamental. As the crude excitement of sporting events may form one group in the community with an appetite for contests or even for war as "news," so the habit of seeking one's enjoyment for one's self, outside the everyday world, may form another group which is less unstable, less homogeneous, more vigorous and not so easily led. Within any large community different groups are formed by the satisfaction of different desires. Such groups may interpenetrate, since quite probably the same youth may go to games and sports and also go out hiking. But nothing is more mistaken than the superficial impression of certain critics that the modern world is forming every one upon the same pattern. The compensations for city life and industrial labor provided by modern transport and the extension of leisure are already permitting a division of men in accordance with their "inner" diversities—the differences of their bodily impulses and of their mental "sets" or tendencies. Leisure used as a means of escape is correcting the evil effects of the pressure of the productive system toward homogeneity of character and outlook; for leisure implies freedom to choose among many different possible ways of escape, and different ways are, in fact, already being explored.

VII

CONVENTIONS AND MODERNITY

REVOLUTIONS are not the most important nor the commonest of social changes. The change through which we are now passing, as indicated in the conditions studied in former chapters, is gradual and not designed; but it is no less fundamental for the future, although it is hardly noticed. The dominant assumptions of earlier generations are quietly displaced by a growth of new habits whose implications are not clearly perceived. The manners of men in converse with women, of adults with children, of the young with the old, of officials with citizens, of educated men and women with foreigners, of those with larger incomes in contact with those who have less—all these have changed, not indeed throughout any community but in significant sections of most modern communities. Manners in streets and shops, the conventions of fellow-travelers and the use of the public provisions for recreation have noticeably changed in the past fifty years. The indications of this change are to be found most easily in a contrast between the illustrated and comic papers of about 1880 and those of 1932. In the half-century which divides those years not only dress and food have changed, not only the most popular entertainments, but the form of manners and the assumptions implied in manners.

Whatever the differences of taste or tendency within any community, the social system remains a whole in so far as conventions govern manners, chiefly in the intercourse of leisure. Those who make a gospel of revolution, as in the French Revolution, introduce new conventions—new modes of address, "citizen" or "comrade," and sometimes new costumes and new forms of public entertainment. But usually conventions are ceremonies or rituals of common life whose origin is forgotten, whose use is unconscious, whose maintenance or disappearance is hardly noticed. The anthropologist who studies the ritual of savages is in danger of "having his leg pulled," if he asks the savages why they follow this or that convention; and no doubt we anthropologists who do "field work" not in Africa but in London and New York, ought not to inquire too deeply into the reasons for the established conventions. The local "savages" are not likely to be conscious of any reason for what they

CONVENTIONS AND MODERNITY

do in their greetings or their common enjoyments. But we may observe certain changes which have taken place in the "tone" of social intercourse as expressed in the appearance of new conventions; and we may note the "inner" change of attitude implied in slight modifications of traditional behavior.

Especially in leisure is the change important. The fact that many more have leisure and opportunities for enjoying it, that many more have variety of clothing and food and control of the decoration of their homes—such facts inevitably cause the formation of new conventions. What, therefore, at first sight appears to be only the passing of old conventions—for example, the older conventional use of "evening dress" for distinguishing an upper class—is fundamentally the development of new conventions, implying a new basis of social intercourse.[1] It may be asked whether the conventions of modernity are merely extensions to larger numbers of the traditional manners or are really new in their form and content. But that could hardly be answered without a much more extensive study of conventions by the anthropologists of civilized life. Con-

---

[1] See correspondence in the London Times, at the end of 1931 and the beginning of 1932, on "evening dress in the stalls" and on the costumes of the fashionable riders in Rotten Row. The disappearance of the old conventions is there noted, long after they have gone.

ventions of greeting—lifting the hat or shaking hands—remain externally the same: but conventions as to the proper subjects of conversation have radically changed. It would be difficult to decide where the old ends and the new begins.

In any case, it must first be recognized that it is useful to have *some* conventions, either old or new, in a civilized society. Joseph Conrad in his story "An Outpost of Progress" speaks of "insignificant and incapable individuals, whose existence is rendered possible only through the high organization of civilized crowds." And he goes on: "Few men realize that their life, the very essence of their character, their capabilities and their audacities, are only the expression of their belief in the safety of their surroundings. The courage, the composure, the confidence; the emotions and principles; every great and every insignificant thought belongs not to the individual but to the crowd; to the crowd that believes blindly in the irresistible force of its institutions and its morals, in the power of its police and of its opinion. But the contact with pure unmitigated savagery, with primitive nature and primitive man, brings sudden and profound trouble into the heart. To the sentiment of being alone of one's kind, to the clear perception of the loneliness of one's thoughts, of one's sensations—to the nega-

CONVENTIONS AND MODERNITY

tion of the habitual which is safe, there is added the affirmation of the unusual, which is dangerous; a suggestion of things vague, uncontrollable and repulsive, whose discomposing intrusion excites the imagination and tries the nerves of the foolish and the wise alike." Conventions are maintained by that sort of fear; but such fear is not, as Conrad seems to imply, objectionable. Fear of being run over is a very good guide in the modern street; and the fear of being left out in the cold by one's fellows is only the reverse side of a desire for their company.

Conventions make us feel "safe" and "at home" with other people; and that feeling is necessary for civilized life. As an example of convention, take clothing. In Western civilization so far men have worn trousers and women skirts; and in all races and times the sexes are conventionally distinguished by their dress. But the actual conventions we use are exactly the opposite of conventions in Eastern countries, where women wear trousers. Other conventions of ours also are opposite to conventions, for example, in China. We nod to indicate "Yes"; but to the Chinese a nod means "No." We sew with the needle moving toward our bodies; the Chinese with it moving away from the body. We shake the other man's hand for a greeting; the Chinese man shakes his own hand, to show that he is pleased to meet you. Indeed it does not matter which you do, so long as everybody round you does the same, so that you both feel safe. That is the use of convention. But in clothing the conventions of our civilization are becoming more unsettled than they have ever been. How long will "Sunday clothes" continue to be used? How long will all men go about disguised as business men, in tubes of dark wool? [2] Conventions of dress and speech and food and manners seem to be spreading to larger numbers; and the very spread of these conventions is changing their form, for they are no longer so obviously used to distinguish between social classes.

But that is so also with the enjoyment of leisure, in ways that were once regarded as the privileges of an "upper class." Not only have the use of the movies and radio, gambling and "hiking" spread to great numbers; but there are also many more games of football played than there were about forty or fifty years ago. Many more women are able and willing to play games; and there are many more places and opportunities for children to play otherwise than in the streets. There has been an increase

[2] It is difficult to say how significant the "nudist" movement is. The freedom from clothes certainly has profound psychological results, which may be beneficial in the destruction of prudery. But a theoretical doctrine easily leads to a new convention—of being unconventional; and it seems likely that the only valid basis for discarding clothes is that one desires to do something interesting enough in itself to make one quite unconscious of any strangeness in discarding them.

CONVENTIONS AND MODERNITY

of the numbers of those who enjoy swimming in the public baths—men and women and children; and a great extension of public parks has taken place during the past half-century. An attempt is now being made to extend the area and variety of great National Parks. Above all, it is important that a new conception of what public parks are for, is beginning to penetrate into the minds of city councilors. In the old days public parks were railed gravel paths between lawns strewn with notices to "keep off the grass." Those with small incomes who could not afford to go into the country, were supposed to keep to the paths; and even in villages, there were no places to play. It is now recognized however that parks should be playgrounds, that walking in a line in your Sunday clothes is not as good as running and jumping on the grass or even walking on it. Whether it is wrong to play games on Sundays in Great Britain has not apparently been decided; but if it is not wrong for the rich, very few will believe that it is wrong for those who are not rich.

As a sign of the times the National Playing Fields Association of Great Britain, which began its work about 1925, should be noted. This association has arranged for gifts of land between 1927 and 1931, amounting to about 3,000 acres, for playing fields;

and the association is represented at an International Recreation Congress, which is held from time to time. The only periodical devoted to the public provision of facilities for games and such forms of recreation, is a monthly called Recreation, published in the United States; but it is evidently recognized in all democratic countries that there should be opportunities for games and play for all; and that has come about within the past thirty years. The convention that the "upper" class should play games or have sports and the others should look on, is gradually breaking down.

Certain ways of using leisure which used to be possible only for a few are now spreading to many. The manners and customs of the few tend to be copied, as dress is copied, when the opportunity to copy arises. That is an old story. That goes on. But something quite different is also happening. In a society which is non-democratic the few tend to change their conventions in order to be distinguished from the many whom they despise; and those who can, escape from among the many by copying the few.[3] But when great numbers have new opportunities, some of them do not copy the

---

[3] I was informed in May 1932 in Oxford by an undergraduate that undergraduates carried umbrellas instead of rain-coats because rain-coats had become common among young men in Oxford who were not undergraduates. "Town" and "Gown" distinctions are forms of snobbery.

"superior" few but make experiments of their own. A new group of conventions arises, which is not derivative but is original. Those who go "hiking" are not copying; they are inventing. Those who play football or other games in public parks are not trying to be "superior"; they are not trying to do what their neighbors cannot do; they are doing what everybody might do. The manners and customs of modern streets are not faded copies of the manners of drawing-rooms. They are manners upon a different basis. The uses of leisure in a democratic society are not merely the non-democratic uses spread more generally. They are different uses; and from them new conventions arise.

The new conventions are arising without any deliberate design. As it was argued above, there is a tendency to make experiments in the modern world. We try new foods and new clothes more often than our grandfathers did. But on the other hand, the food of the country and the town is becoming more similar; the food of one country is adopted in another; and as for clothes, in a voyage to Berlin from London through Belgium and Holland, one cannot tell, from the clothes of the men at the stations, what country one is in. Even the East and Africa are beginning to dress like America; and in England the clothes to be seen in Manchester are exactly like those to be seen in London. In the occupations of leisure millions in all parts of the country and in many different countries are going to the movies. They are doing the same things to amuse themselves. Their habits and attitudes are, therefore, in one sense more "conventional," because what is done and thought in moving pictures is the same over larger areas of experience. How far any conventions will spread, it may not be possible to say. Shaking hands is common among us and it astonishes a Chinese or Japanese. But they may begin to do it, if they see American films. On the other hand, we shall probably not adopt the manners of the warrior of New Guinea simply because we have seen them "in·the pictures." However, suppose that a list were made of the commonest conventions in our own country—such as shaking hands, or taking off your hat to a lady, or kissing as a sign of affection, or saying that it is a fine day—the question is, What difference, if any, have the changes of the past thirty years made in such customs? For answer you must go into the streets and shops and movie theaters and notice what people do.

It has been remarked in an earlier chapter that moving pictures have increased the knowledge of

CONVENTIONS AND MODERNITY

the majority as to how other people behave in other social circles and in other nations. This has weakened the hold of local conventions. But other changes have occurred which are not due to the movies. The fact that education is more general and on a higher level than it was, has changed the manners of those who use tea-shops and buses toward waitresses and bus-conductors. The traditional attitude toward persons serving you implied the kind condescension of a master toward an inferior. A "superior" person ordering food is distinguishable from us common folk; and I am sorry to say that this "superior" manner is used on the stage in America as if it were typical of the Englishman. But the new conventions indicate that the person serving you is not felt to be an inferior, nor a piece of machinery. Your manner to the bus-conductor and his to you are different from the traditional; indeed perhaps the new convention may imply exactly the contrary of the old—namely, that the person serving is, in some way, superior to the person served.

Conventions remain in the modern world; but new conventions are taking the place of the old. The conventions of an aristocratic society are passing away. The conventions of a community of equals are replacing those of a community of dependents and their controllers; for democratic manners may seem to be bad manners, but they are certainly different manners. Let me explain by examples.

Manners in America may seem to be bad or good, according to the standard adopted by the critic, but at any rate they are the manners of a society of equals. When I was lecturing at an American University I used, after my lecture, to take lunch at a club where the waiters and waitresses were students who had been attending my lectures. They did not expect my manners in addressing them to be different in the dining-room from what they were in the class-room; and I certainly would have had no objection to serving their meal, after having lectured to them. In neither case were the manners of superior and inferior applicable. We were equals in whatever relation to one another our work of the moment placed us. In France also the conventions are those of a democratic society. One says "Madame" to the postmistress, as well as to the rich lady with nothing to do. But in Great Britain . . . perhaps I had better not say anything about snobbery and its counterpart, flunkeyism. I might seem to be impolite to those who do not understand what I am talking about; and those who understand, will not require further descriptions of the traditional manners. There are some who think that certain people ought to touch their caps to the squire and the parson—and clearly, so they ought, but only in reply, because the squire and the parson ought to touch theirs. In France I should not dream of asking a policeman the way, without touching my hat and addressing him as "Monsieur." But manners even in England—if one is to judge from the streets and the shops—are beginning to be the manners of equals in a society of equals.

Another sign of change in convention is that manners are much more "impersonal" than they used to be. It is undeniable that the change from village streets or even small-town streets to the city area has caused a change in the influence of neighbors. In a village every one knows when Mrs. Smith quarrels with Mrs. Brown; and the village becomes still more interested if Mrs. Smith quarrels with Mr. Smith. Gossip is the news of a village; and much more interesting news it is than most of what is in the newspapers. Indeed when there is no gossip, the majority do not find any substitute for it in the discussion of large questions of public policy. Perhaps they ought to be "political animals." Perhaps one ought to greet one's friends with "How is the Pound Sterling to-day?" or "Is the dear Gold Standard keeping up his spirits?" But it may be excusable occasionally to ask, "Well, has any one run away with Mrs. Smith yet?"—on the assumption, of course, that this Mrs. Smith was looking about for some one to run away with her. In America this is called "the personal touch"; and the newspapers in America attempt to provide village gossip, for the public mind in America is still largely the "small town" mind; and because it is difficult to find gossip about one's neighbors in city areas, gossip survives upon movie stars.

The commonest subject in talking to your friends remains the interest in the people you know. But in a village one knows every other villager; and in a city area one is lost among innumerable indistinguishable people, catching buses or trains and going to multiple shops where the shop-girls seem to be only machines, quite unlike the village shopkeeper who retails local scandals with tea and sugar. But, as I know less about other people, even my friends, in a city area, so other people know less about me. The control of public opinion over one's daily action is not so close; and the result is a new kind of convention. This new convention assumes that the person you meet is an equal; for it is too dangerous to assume superiority if you do not know from manner, dress, or speech, what position the person you meet may hold. At work, the position of most people, with respect to those they work with, is obvious; but in leisure nobody knows what social functions the other person may perform. The result is a change of manners in streets and shops which is far more important than any change in the drawing-rooms of the few. The new manners are more "free and easy," less obviously formal, much more individual and much less those of any social class. Therefore although something may have been lost in the disappearance of the village gossip, which used at least to make people known to to one another personally, in our more impersonal age we have gained at least this—the manners of a society of equals.

Not more than a beginning has been made in Great Britain; other countries seem to be more advanced in this and therefore to be more civilized; but comparisons between nations as wholes are generally misleading. The new conventions of equality in the modern world are promoted by the extension of leisure to those who have to work during most of their waking lives, by the form of entertainment during leisure—the radio, the movies, and the new habit of "hiking," by the extension of the facilities for games and by the new ways of going about, as in buses. All this is producing a social revolution in "culture" or the forms of civilized life; and this revolution is being made inevitable by the new education.

Into this new world of more democratic and more impersonal manners a new generation is entering. Children are very conventional. If any one of them is, in fact, original, it is by accident and without intention. I know an American lady, living in a small town in New England, whose little daughter of four or five wanted to play in the garden in her bathing-suit, as it was a hot summer. The good lady told her little daughter that she could do so; but must on no account go across the road to see her friends in her bathing-suit. Half an hour after, the little girl was seen crossing the road with her bathing-suit carefully folded under her arm and nothing on at all. She was only too willing to be conventional, although she slightly misunderstood the convention. Even children's games are conventional, for many of them are very early forms of ritual. When a child asks for a "new" game, all it wants is a different old game. And there never are such conventional marriages and funerals as those that occur in nurseries or in children's play in the streets. Indeed all the basis of human intercourse is convention; and children know well enough that it does not matter what you do, so long as you do what the people you meet expect you to do. But the problem of the modern world is that conventions are changing; and the child may be injured in the process. It has been well said that a city is no place for children. City pavements are not good playgrounds; and city streets, where the milk comes in tins or bottles, are not so good for children as the lane to the village, where the cows come in for milking. But cities are not good for children most of all because in them tradition and convention are confused or insecure or superficial. In the new world which is growing up in the midst of the old, we need dignity in age and, in childhood, grace of movement and manner. Therefore the children at play or going to the movies should be making for themselves new manners, for the modern world will depend just as much upon modern manners as upon modern machinery.

It is necessary to look below the forms and ceremonies we use in our contact with other people to see the soul of the form, the spirit underlying the ritual. It would be foolish deliberately to destroy or weaken conventions; but it is wise to know it for what it is. We need not cease to shake hands for greeting, nor to bow to one another, even when we feel that these forms are only the arbitrary signs of much more important sensations and attitudes. It was said long ago that "manners makyth man," but what we have to recognize as important in the modern world is that "man makyth manners"—that is to-day, that the conventions and uniformities which are useful are those which are not substitutes for deeper emotions and finer attitudes, but are the natural and generally recognized signs of such emotions and attitudes.

The traditional view of "manners," especially in the "good form" which became a sort of fetish worship in British public schools, overestimates the importance of the ritual and underestimates the value of what it may express or develop. The most elaborate manners or politeness in history is to be found in eighteenth-century France. The form of civilization then established provided that one should bow or curtsey at the right time at a particular angle; but such a civilization was hardly a step above the civilization of an African kingdom whose king has to be served by the mutilations of his subjects. Forms and ceremonies in social intercourse tend to survive long after the intention or attitude which gave rise to them has disappeared, and old forms can, up to a certain point, be used to embody a new attitude—just as an old language can be used to express new ideas. But the first step in freeing ourselves from an obsolete attitude of mind is to escape from the superstition that the form is what matters. The modern world is creating its own code of manners. The new conventions are less rigid and much more light-hearted than the proprieties of the nineteenth century; and some old people complain that the younger generation has no manners because these old people know only the old manners and in any case overrate the importance of any manners at all.

If conventions of some sort are useful in civilized life and if the new conventions in social intercourse are the results of an undesigned tendency toward equality in modern life, we may either support or obstruct that tendency by public policy or personal action. Probably there is not enough evidence to show whether, in Great Britain, support or obstruction is strongest. In any case the majority of people drift and have no definite ideas about the sort of lives they would like to lead. They feel perhaps that, whatever sort of life they would prefer, they "can't do anything about it." They *feel* enslaved, even if in fact they are not. They wait for something to happen, when they could make it happen, if they knew their own strength. Here then is one of the problems of leisure in modern life. The attitude of men in company with others in leisure and the expression of that attitude in manners and customs—these are the forces which transform society. In leisure most men and women are in reality freer than they think they are. They could invent instead of copying. They could, without any revolutionary gospel, begin in their own persons the transformation of a society in the direction of democracy, not by merely opposing the old conventions but by laying the foundation for new ones. But whether there is any conscious direction of the form of manners or even any conscious change of "inner" attitude expressed in manners—that seems doubtful.

VIII

LEISURE AND THE WOMAN'S MOVEMENT

LEISURE has been traditionally assumed to be an opportunity not merely for entertainment but also for the deliberate consideration and control of public affairs. In the slave societies of the ancient world, in Athens and in the Roman Empire, the few citizens, no doubt, believed that they used their leisure in the control of public affairs partly for the sake of the women and the slaves, who were believed to be naturally incapable of thus using leisure. In the oligarchic societies of the eighteenth century and the first half of the nineteenth century in Europe and America, the "gentlemen" who belonged to a leisured class, no doubt, conceived their control of public policy to be beneficial to the "ladies" and the "working" men, who had not the noble propensity of gentlemen to use leisure so well.

A certain resistance even to-day to the extension of leisure for women and for workers in industry may be the result of an unconscious desire to retain the privilege of using leisure for the control of public affairs by a small leisured class. Not that those who have the privilege are self-seeking! Indeed they probably believe quite seriously that public affairs will not be properly conducted, if any one else conducts them.

Aristotle was probably honest in his argument that women and slaves were not quite human enough to be "political"; for the history of social development is not a mere record of oppressors struggling to retain advantages for themselves until they are overcome. The psychological facts are more complex. The beneficiaries of any social system probably believe that they can "run" any system better than those who bear most of its burdens. Leisure, however, has recently increased and the uses of leisure have recently become more numerous for all and sundry. As far back as the 1850's the shortening of working hours gave the workers under the industrial system not only opportunity for rest and enjoyment but also surplus energy to look around them—to see the general lines of the system of which their own lives formed a part. At first the surplus energy affecting public affairs found its chief outlet in the religion of the chapels, where public speaking and spontaneous coöperation for public purposes were learnt. Later the traditional subjection was questioned, in the application to public affairs of that same Gospel which had been made the bulwark of authority; and the leisure which had been used for religion and for mutual help began to be used in efforts to obtain a share of political power.

Within the past fifty years one of the most significant social changes resulting from an extension of leisure has been the growth of a variety of groups claiming political rights. Leisure, hardly won from long hours of work, is now used by great numbers in public meetings, in discussion of public affairs and in voluntary unpaid activities for the reform of inherited evils.[1] The incidental effects of the new uses of leisure for entertainment, which have been discussed above, have not had greater social influence than the deliberate use of leisure in the attempts to control public policy. These organized efforts may be called "social movements." The effect upon public affairs of this use of leisure by those who work for a living is not likely to be the same as that of control by "leisured classes." The social system of the Greek city state would have been very differently described if, not Aristotle and Plato, but a slave or a woman had provided us with evi-

[1] Under this heading comes the social movement for "adult education" in all its many forms. But the use of the leisure of workers in this movement goes back to the 1830's.

dence. The doctrine of later times that progress is necessarily slow is not so easily accepted by those who suffer if reforms are delayed. When therefore the immense majority who work with their hands have leisure and energy to spare for the consideration of public affairs, quite new situations arise.

While men and women are at work in order to get what they need, they have to fit into the system of society as it stands. The man who is building a house and the woman who is cooking a dinner or washing the children, do not usually have energy to spare, while they are at work, for looking at the work they are doing "from the outside"—for seeing it "in its setting" and for thinking how it may be improved. One at least of the uses of leisure for those who work is that in leisure a man or a woman may stand aside and *look*—not merely stand aside as a way of "escaping" in entertainment—but stand aside and *look*. But when in leisure you look from the outside at your work—at its place in the social system and your place in that system, you may desire to change that place or to change, in one respect or another, the social system. You may want to resist the new tendencies which seem to you destructive of what is most valuable in life. For example, some of those who have written letters to me about what I said in radio talks, were very angry about motor-cars and about children going to movies. They thought that the evil effects of new inventions were more important than the good.

On the other hand, some of those who stand aside and look, see evils remaining over from earlier times. Such people tend to support recent changes which have undermined old evils; and they may over-estimate the amount of good in the new world, just as others over-estimate the evil. But in either case in leisure people adopt attitudes toward "the whole show"; and social movements arise— not merely political and economic movements, but movements for changing education or art or medicine. In the widest sense of the word, "citizenship" is the attention to public affairs which arises, *generally in leisure,* out of our attitude toward what we and our neighbors do. What each of us does affects others and what others do affects us—that is all we mean by "public affairs": they are my affairs seen in their setting. The changes of the past thirty years have caused new controversies, new attitudes and new desires; and all these flourish and blossom in the new leisure. Leisure in fact is used for attending meetings and discussions of public affairs and for the organization of new groups to oppose or to promote new ideas.

One outstanding example of recent change resulting from a social movement is the new position of women. This, no doubt, is partly due to industrial changes such as new kinds of machinery and the desire for new kinds of product. I am not thinking only of repetition processes and automatic machinery, which have made work easier for women, but also of such new machinery as the typewriter and the telephone which have made more work possible for women. Thousands of women can now make independent incomes for themselves. But there have been changes also in what women do when they are not working for a living. These changes are clearly in part due to tendencies not deliberately designed to alter the position of women —such as the use of lighter material for clothing, and the increase of entertainment for women in the movie and radio. But the most important change is due to the deliberate effort of a few men and women who were determined to improve the social status of women. In very general terms, they desired to alter the traditional position which was one of dependence so as to secure a new position of equality.

How far, then, has the position of women been altered from one of dependence to one of equality during the past fifty years? Clearly changes which had begun before 1900 are not yet completed. It is not implied that all women were dependent before 1900, nor that most women are treated as equals of men to-day; but there has been a noticeable approach toward equality since 1900, which is due both to the new ways in which women use leisure for entertainment and also to the deliberate use of leisure for changing their position in public affairs. There is no need to be reminded of the history of the suffrage movement before the war; but we should note that in most advanced countries women had no vote in 1900 nor in 1910. Since 1918 in Great Britain women over thirty have had the vote; and, since 1928 only, women have had the vote on the same terms as men. This is the result of a deliberate effort made by comparatively small groups of women in Western countries. But the same movement is to be found in Turkey and China and India. All over the world the old assumption, on which male control of public affairs rested, has been undermined; and women have gained some political power, if not yet equal power with men.

I am not concerned here with the political effects of women's use of the vote. Perhaps it has made no difference to the kinds of view which are represented by different groups of voters; but the evidence from Germany, which is the only country where the woman's vote is distinguished from the man's, shows that most women are in the central groups between the extremes of the Right and the Left. It is sometimes said, therefore, that women exercise a moderating influence. Much more likely is the suggestion that policies which are concerned with food and health are attractive to women, and policies which have to do with prestige or national power are attractive to men. Women in our civilization seem to think in terms which are more definite, real or concrete, and men tend to mythological beliefs. Men are "practical," as Mencken argues in his "Defence of Women," only in those trivial matters of calculation which are useful in trade. They are not "practical" in personal problems of daily life. However, even to compare women and men in such general terms is a sign that our civilization is still somewhat primitive. We cannot be said to know what women could do in a society in which they had had for some generations the same political and social experience as men have had. All attempts to find biological or psychological grounds for existing differences between men and women, under-estimate the importance of social conventions; for the traditional conventions imply the assumption of the inferiority of women—an assumption which still has great influence in practice, although some approach to equality between men and women has been made recently.

Again, the approach to equality in public affairs has been accompanied by a rapid improvement in women's *education* during the past fifty years. The schools have already made much better provision for women's education: the universities are less medieval—even in Great Britain, where the so-called "older" universities still claim the medieval privilege of old age in opposing new ideas. Adult education—which includes women's education—has made progress; and in addition to what is strictly called "education," there are Women Citizens' Associations and Women Institutes, both for the use of leisure and both very successful in support of the tendency to equality for women. Equality should not be confused with similarity. Nobody supposes that women should become men. A Women Citizens' Association is not intended to make women think about public affairs exactly as men do—but rather to make them able to contribute to public affairs their own point of view, their own kinds of ability and intelligence. In the United States it is the Women Citizens' Groups which have arranged for the discussion of public affairs on the radio; because so many women prefer to stay at home instead of attending public meetings. But the purpose is simply to bring into the common store of thought and action about public affairs any intelligence and ability which happens to exist among them.

Similarly the Women's Institutes, not only in Great Britain but also in the Dominions, have rapidly increased in numbers and influence in the past twenty years; and although they are concerned partly with women's occupations, chiefly under non-urban conditions, they are also concerned with provision for leisure. They have been the means for introducing to women many new interests and new ways of using leisure.

Among younger women, and perhaps in connection with new methods in the schools, there has been a great increase in games and athletics. The change is more striking in such countries as Germany, where girls used to be kept from any vigorous exercise and are now encouraged to play games. But among us too there is more tennis-playing, more swimming and running for girls and younger women. I am not thinking of the "ladies of leisure" who do nothing else. I am thinking of typists and workers in chocolate factories and waitresses and textile workers. There is much more opportunity than ever before for women to use their leisure as men always have. And this is the result of deliberate support given to these activities for women.

I need not do more than glance at certain other signs of equality in the use of leisure for women and men. The moving pictures tend to promote enjoyment for women and men together as contrasted with the separateness of earlier entertainments. The radio provides entertainment which men and women enjoy together. Betting too has been shown in an earlier chapter to have spread among women, as it has among men. I am not approving of this nor condemning it. For the present I note only the tendency to equality in the uses of leisure; for, indeed, the position of women *in leisure* seems to have changed much more in the past fifty years than the position of women in the work they do.

The social tendency so far described gives rise to a social movement, either in reaction against it or in the effort to promote it. Clearly there may be many different views about what *ought* to be the position of women in society; but two opposing views may be selected, in order that what is called "the Woman's Movement" may be understood as a social force. On the one hand, it may be said that women are so different from men that the best development of what there is in them, in body and mind, should be on the lines of tradition. Some women bear children; and no men can. The family group is dependent upon a peculiarly intimate connection of the wife with the home. In the vast majority of cases, the married man earns income by services outside his home; and therefore his training, his attitude, his influence upon the system outside his home ought to be quite different from his wife's. Not every one indeed is married; and not every one ought to be married. But the position of women with respect to men is fundamentally dependent upon the sexual relationship; and this implies a quite different, not necessarily superior and inferior, morality for women and men. That is the traditional view. It is notorious, although it is denied by traditionalists, that the operative moral standard in the past implied a much laxer practice in sexual relationships for men as compared with women. But if the difference of the sexes is what the traditionalist supposes, then the modern tendency to equality of status and moral standards may be regarded as dangerous.[2] Nobody denies that some change in the old order is desirable. Nobody believes that women ought to be household slaves or merely instruments of the pleasures or the careers

---

[2] The most extreme recent statement of the traditionalist view of the position of women is in the present Pope's Encyclical on Marriage.

of men. But some would say that the unsettlement of the traditional family relationships and the new moral standards applied to personal relationship between the sexes are causing more evil than good. By that is meant, not merely discomfort but an actual degradation of what is finest in men and women. That is the case against supporting or praising recent tendencies.

On the other hand, some people (not, indeed, only women) support the recent changes in the position of women and desire more of them. They regard the traditional relationship between men and women as, in its chief features, obsolete and objectionable—not merely in politics and working life but also in leisure and in everyday customs. In the support for tendencies to equality—in the effort to give to women more of the opportunities which men have had, it is implied that we are building up not merely new customs but *new ideals* of what men and women ought to be. Those who support the new tendencies imply that civilization can hardly be said to exist until the equality of men and women is taken for granted, and that the various slightly comic arguments against the vote for women, surviving from an earlier barbarism, to the effect that women have less strength or that some women bear children at certain intervals, are hardly worth remembering.[3] None of the differences between men and women prove anything with regard to the equality of rights which is now, at any rate, theoretically granted in modern civilization. The modernists say that in spite of the partial success of the Women's Movement, many inequalities, in practice, remain. The jungle of ancient habits and customs, in some cases embodied in law, is still obstructive, although clearing has been made in the forest.

Many problems of modern life, however, in the relations of men and women, seem to arise from the fact that nobody quite knows what this new principle of equality means, in terms of daily habits and customs. I have heard men and women, who would claim to be "modern" at least in assuming equality, speaking and acting in the old way—the man, if he is a husband, treating his wife as a personal servant, and the woman, if she is a wife, accepting what amounts to "orders." But if there is equality of the partners in marriage, then there is no "head of the family." The woman's work, whatever it is, inside or outside of the house, is not merely nor mainly for the sake of the man's career, as the man's is not only for the sake of the woman.

[3] The French Senate remembers these arguments about once every year and thereupon rejects any discussion of a Bill to give the franchise to women.

There are survivals of old status in the idea that a man has a career or a public function to perform, to which the woman contributes support or assistance; but it is a question here of modern ideals, not of the actual structure of society. The same habits and customs can be viewed in entirely different ways. A woman may continue to cook or buy food and clothing, and the man may continue to run a railway-engine or an office, and yet the whole situation may change if one sort of work is not thought to be superior to the other. Apart entirely from the relations between a husband and wife, the position of women as cooks, or domestic servants, or school-teachers, should not be inferior nor less important socially. From the "modern" point of view this book is partly the result of the work of the person who cooked my food: it is not "mine" in the sense of being created out of nothing by a superior being. What you are now reading was once mutton and potatoes; and they became me after they were worked at by those who made such things digestible. I am not "superior" to the person who made it possible for me to do what I am now doing. That is a quite general principle—but it has a special bearing upon the position of women; for there is an ancient tradition that the work women do is somehow inferior or less important than what men do. What is women's work as contrasted with what is men's work, is dependent upon ancient custom; and the custom differs in different races and at different stages in the life of any race. Thus in marriage, among us, there are certain fixed customs as to the position of husband and wife in the work of maintaining the household, but into these customs we are beginning to introduce new conceptions of equality.

The more fundamental change however is in the personal relationship of husband and wife, in sexual matters and other similar issues. We are in the midst of a change that is world-wide. Turkish women, for example, as well as European and American women are discussing and using new methods of birth-control. Certainly in Europe and America the change is affecting the younger men and women. For one thing, there is much more frankness in the discussion of sexual relationships, both between married couples and otherwise. Younger men and women are much readier to discuss sexual relationships than similar people were, fifty years ago. Indeed we seem to have recovered from the first excitement of novelty in such discussions. It is no longer regarded as astonishing or "advanced" to speak plainly and with modern conceptions of psychology for our guidance. We are "settling down" to new assumptions as the basis for our conduct; and among these is, first, the assumption that nothing can be right for a man—or even excusable—which is not right or excusable for a woman. Further, it is assumed in those circles which have been at all touched by modern ideas, that in marriage it is the wife and not the husband who must finally decide how many children she will have and when. The physical as well as the economic and social reasons for this, appeal strongly to modern minds. But that part of life which can, without too great an extension of meaning, be called "sexual" is obviously concerned with very much more than merely having children. Some companionships between men and women which are obviously of this nature do not involve marriage or having children. But here we are at the beginning of a new kind of civilization. Indeed perhaps we are beginning to see that a wife who is only a wife is a bore, as a husband who is only a husband is generally a beast. Every civilized person, it is argued, at least in the modern world, should have not only many interests, but also many different kinds of personal contacts outside the home; and that improves the home. It is implied in this new view of the home that the "doll wife," as portrayed in Ibsen's "Doll's House," who is still to be found in some houses modern enough for radio-sets, is obsolete. China shepherdesses are all very well on a mantelpiece, but not on the floor. And as for the strong, silent man—perhaps in modern conditions an intelligent woman might suspect that he was silent because he had nothing to say. In any case, equality seems to require greater intelligence and more subtlety in the relationship between men and women. That clearly affects the situation outside marriage. Many more women are independent economically, many more educated to think for themselves, and many more free to use leisure as they please; and therefore the "tone" of social intercourse between at least younger men and women should be much more that of a companionship of equals. Such is the argument of those who support the tendencies of to-day which are changing the old position of women.

It is possible that many of those who suppose themselves to be "advanced" in their views as to the proper relationship of the sexes, are not aware how far the principles they accept would carry them in practice. Many of those who approve of votes for women or even of economic freedom for women, would shrink from the changes necessary in our standards of morality if we were to take seriously what is meant by freedom. But clearly the so-called Woman's Movement implies a change which is deeper down in the social structure than either politics or economic organization can reach. That is why the real issue is generally faced only when controversies arise as to the religious traditions in this or that circle. The opposition to the new tendency is expressed not only in the recent encyclical of the Pope on marriage, but also in the advocacy of a rapid birth-rate—one of the traditional methods of enslavement for women, in the restriction of public games or gymnastics for women and in the traditional suspicion of coeducation. On the other hand, the new tendency is experimental. It is recognized that we have had no experience in the past of a civilization based upon equality and that the implications, if not the actual statements of the traditional moral teachers, are obsolete in matters affecting the relation between the sexes. But experiment is not blind groping: it is action under the guidance of deliberate thought, tested, as to its results, by reference to a conscious purpose. For example, the form of intimacy in any particular case may vary from casual conversation to continuous coöperation in a common task; and the results may be either a deterioration or an expansion of vitality and personality. In a region in which most of the great discoveries have still to be made, rules are not good guides.

Recent social movements, of which the Woman's Movement is one example, have developed largely because of the extension of leisure to new sections of the community. But they are not yet powerful enough. The greater attention to public affairs of persons whose ancestors left such affairs to their "betters" is not everywhere welcomed. Indeed some plans for the provision of entertainment in the leisure of those who work are—perhaps unconsciously—intended to supply a substitute for thinking or action with regard to public policy. "Bread and circuses" was not, even in ancient Rome, the choice of the populace; it was what they were given to keep them quiet. But the tendency to use spare time for the reform of a social system has already gone too far to be resisted successfully.

IX

CHILDREN'S LEISURE

THE new generation is never left to itself in any age or country, even in its leisure. Inevitably the world is an adult world, into which children enter; and their ideas as well as their customs, their education and their leisure, are deeply influenced by a social system to which they are strangers. But within the past half-century changes have occurred in the relation of children to adults, especially in their leisure.

Play is no longer regarded as waste of time. Indeed educational method has been almost transformed by the study of children's play. Also there is a very general belief that the child should express its own opinions and make its own attempts at learning or enjoyment. The old conception that "to spare the rod is to spoil the child" is obsolete; and nobody now expects a child to be seen and not heard. Legal provision is now made in all civilized countries, not only to protect the child from economic exploitation, even by its own parents, but also to secure for the child adequate food and bodily care. Indeed it has been said that we are living in "the century of the child."

The larger issue—the relation of the adult world to childhood, however, does not concern us here. For our purpose it will be enough to note the new uses of leisure by children and the social effects of these new uses—the effect, for example, of moving pictures and radio. These have changed the playtime of children almost by accident, for it was some years after the introduction of the new mechanisms for entertainment that their effect on children was perceived to be important.

But the use of leisure by children has not in fact been left to the accidental effects of new inventions. There have been social movements in the past fifty years, which express a deliberate policy of changing either the experience of childhood or the new world which will arise when those who are now children are men and women. Obviously education in school is not the only means of preparing for that future world. The habits and attitudes of the new generation of 1932, acquired during leisure—whether at play or dreaming, will be projected into the social system of 1950. The Fascists in Italy and the Communists in Russia have this in view, in their provision for the leisure of children; but even in the less "organized" leisure of the democratic tradition, attempts are made to direct the use of leisure by children. Thus the leisure of children nowadays is a field for one kind of social movement—the deliberate attempt to form the dominant social tone of twenty or thirty years hence. Two quite distinct new issues therefore should be discussed: first, the unintended effect upon children of the new machines for entertainment, and secondly, the deliberate attempt to form the mind of twenty or thirty years hence, by directing the use of the leisure of children to-day.

Before considering, however, the leisure of children, some reference ought to be made to the changed position of children in the modern world, which is due to the fact that there are *fewer of them* in proportion to the number of adults. An abnormal and sudden decrease of births and an increase of deaths of children took place in Europe and in Great Britain from 1914 to 1918; and that abnormal decrease in the number of children is now affecting the schools. There are fewer children at school now than there would have been if no European war had occurred. There will soon be a decrease in the proportion of the youthful, also due to the war, when the children of to-day become the youths of to-morrow. But that is not the most fundamental change of the past thirty years. The immediate effects of the World War will pass away. Clearly, if we are to have another great war, the abnormal decrease in youth will occur again. Children may then become so few that they will be kept as rarities. Already it is suggested that, in the next war, babies will have to be kept in gas-tight dug-outs. But that may be considered later!

At the moment the most fundamental change in the position of children in Western civilization is due to the general fall in the birth-rate which is not due to the World War but to permanent conditions of modern life. Since the 1880's in northwestern Europe the birth-rate has fallen from about thirty per thousand to about nineteen per thousand; and the fall is similar in the United States and in the British Dominions. Meantime, improved diet, medicine, and sanitation have made it possible for adults to live longer and therefore a greater number of people over forty or fifty years of age are now alive. Again, older people are more vigorous now than they used to be. In Shakspere's time a man was in old age at fifty—"sans teeth, sans eyes . . . sans everything." That is the dismal picture of old age in "As You Like It." But now men and women of over fifty still dance and sing vigorously. Not only are children fewer than they were in proportion to the number of adults, but also they count less, in so far as adults are more vigorous. "Counting less" also means in economic terms not being necessary for increasing the family income; and therefore children in the homes of wage-earners are probably nowadays freer to play than they were in the past because more adults are earning incomes.

Further, increased knowledge has reduced the death-rate of children, so that the smaller number now born have a greater chance of survival; and those that survive are more vigorous than children were in the Middle Ages, or than they are now in more primitive societies. On the whole, therefore, children not being so much needed as workers, their greater health and vitality can find expression in leisure; and besides, being fewer and stronger than in old days, they are more likely to be given special consideration and more likely to go their own way. The family with four or five children has become in Great Britain, Germany, and Scandinavia, a rarity; and the family with one or two children only is common. The effect of this on the character and outlook of children is immense; for children who grow up in large families differ from children in small families in their outlook as well as in their social habits.

The increase in the number of adults, able to earn their own living in normal times, should mean a much smaller number of "dependents" in society—either children or the aged. And as the family income has to provide for fewer, more of the family income will be spent upon what used to be called "luxuries." These luxuries are mainly entertainments for leisure; and the children share in the larger proportion of time and energy and money, which is thus available. The fewer children of to-day, as compared with those of forty or fifty years ago, will naturally have more leisure and more opportunities for using it. In terms of economic science, expenditure on "necessaries" will be smaller in proportion to the expenditure on "luxuries." Boys and girls will be accustomed to spending on enjoyment—which is an advance in civilization. I am thinking, as you will understand, of the great majority of boys and girls, who are sons and daughters of manual workers. These have not had, in earlier times, much opportunity for enjoying their time out of school; and it is an advance in civilization if they are able to spend energy and money on more than food and clothing. But the change in the proportion of persons dependent upon each family income gives more opportunity for children to use their leisure enjoyably.

In the midst of the biological, psychological, and economic changes, due to a falling birth-rate, have come—the movies. Thousands of children from quite poor homes go to "the pictures" every week; and children from all sorts of homes thus get impressions of an adult world which was quite unknown to former generations of children—to us, in fact, when we were children. Two views are possible as to the effect of the films on children. Some say that it is bad. Students of "child psychology" have discussed the effect of film-pictures upon the eyes of children; some have thought that the excitement which children can have nowadays is forming a society with a passion for excitement. If that is so, then political leaders will have a new kind of instrument in the people of the future —more pliable, more changeable and much more easily led. On the other hand, it is possible to argue that the films provide an outlet for the desire for excitement; and that that desire is relieved or rendered less dangerous by being expended in vicarious adventure. Looking on at violence, for example, may be a substitute for being violent, not an inducement to be so. No evidence that I have seen is adequate for showing what is the general effect of moving pictures upon children. Obviously the effect is important, but much more careful collection of evidence is necessary before any clear conclusion can be reached. It is always easy to condemn what is new, especially if one is ignorant of what happened in the good old days; but the experience of children in streets and homes, before the days of the movies, was by no means so good that we can afford to lament the coming of a new kind of experience. It is not always the case that one jumps from the frying-pan into the fire; for even a sausage sometimes jumps clear. Some children are injured by the films; but others are improved by them. Also, it is quite possible that the effect upon children is far less important than we think it, those of us who were not children when the moving picture first appeared. The radio, for example, has not as great an imaginative effect upon children, who have found it a normal part of their world, as it has upon those who were adults before it became common. It still seems to me rather strange to "turn on" Toulouse or Berlin; but a small boy I know seems to think it quite commonplace. So also moving pictures are perhaps taken for granted by children, and are therefore less impressive.

This conclusion, however, is warranted—that

the cinema has not yet been adjusted to the thought and imagination of children. It is not only that it should be used more, educationally; but even for entertainment in leisure, the films could provide very much more for the needs of children.[1] There is no reason why there should not be children's movies. Again, we do not know yet how far the "talkie" will extend the effect of the old silent films; but obviously a new language may be learnt by children, just as they are learning a special pronunciation from the radio. In some parts of England children refer to good English as "speaking wireless"; and this new speech may overcome one of the obstacles which divide Great Britain into social castes—namely, the differences of accent and intonation among children with different family incomes.

There may be disagreement about these new uses of leisure for children. Some will say that films of any sort are disturbing to children; others will say that there ought to be special films for children; and there may be some who say that what might be bad for children on the films "slides off them" without affecting them so much as adults tend to suppose. It is difficult for adults to allow

---

[1] See Report "Sound Films in Schools" published by The Schoolmaster, London, Eng. Various proposals have been made for children's moving pictures and some have been actually established.

for the fact that what has meaning for them may have no meaning at all for children. In any case, the cinema affects children well or ill, without any definite action being taken to control its effects.

Let us turn now to the provisions that have been made deliberately for the good of boys and girls in their leisure. Clearly the increase of playgrounds has been important; and in public parks one sees nowadays corners in which boys and girls can find things to play with. The National Playing Fields Association in Great Britain deals with the needs of adults, as well as those of children; but the children have derived most benefit from the space now provided for their play. The same principle could be extended. There is no reason why large halls, heated and lighted, should not be used by children in the winter months. Even in our parks we are still suffering from the nineteenth-century conception of an "open space" in a city, as a space into which nobody goes. There are still thousands of so-called Squares and Gardens, carefully fenced off lest any one should do any more than look at them; but the modern conception of grass is that it should be walked on and of trees that they should be leaned against. The sort of "Nature" that is inside a fence has no value. But perhaps no open space in a city area is good enough for children; and the modern education authorities therefore provide city children with journeys to the country. How limited the world of city children is can hardly be realized by those with larger incomes; but in the L.C.C. pamphlet on "School Journeys" it is noted that five girls in the top class of a London school saw a live cow for the first time when they were about fourteen, in 1928. Children in city areas are too far separated from nature; but an effort has been made in the past thirty years to remedy this evil.

Another great change of the past fifty years in the use of leisure by children is the social movement embodied in the Boy Scouts and the Girl Guides. This movement has been consciously directed for the use of leisure by children; but it is obviously much less narrow in its general influence than certain similar movements in countries under dictatorships. Both in Italy and in Russia the leisure of children is organized consciously with a view to transforming society. The balilla in Italy is designed to make a future generation of Fascists; and the very young Communists of Russia learn in their leisure to oppose capitalism. But in our less organized form of society boys and girls are so far not consciously influenced in their playtime except in an effort to maintain traditional loyalties.

The Scout movement represents not merely a new use of leisure but an outlook and attitude which it is sought to establish in the new generation by this new use of leisure; and this outlook and attitude, so far as it is consciously expressed by the directors and organizers of the movement, is largely conventional, although some attempt is made to modernize patriotism and ecclesiastical religion. But what actually happens to boys and girls through "scouting" is more important than what the directors of the movement would like to happen. From this point of view, the Scout movement represents two effects of new uses of the leisure of children—first, the closer contact with nature, and secondly, companionship in adventure. Boy Scouts and Girl Guides spend their spare time in a return to more simple conditions, at any rate in play. It is a much more genuine experience than they could have by reading adventure stories. The badges and rules and sacred codes of Scouts and Guides are similar to the secret rites and customs of all "gangs" or groups of children. Thousands of boys and girls have learnt from the Scout movement to track and to hide and to camp in the open, and so far this movement seems to have been much less dominated by adults than similar movements have been hitherto. Again, a return to simpler natural conditions involves also simpler social conditions; and the Scouts and Guides have contrived, so far, to unite boys and girls of families with different social standings. In Great Britain it is wonderful that even a little has been done in this direction; but that little tells in the direction of releasing a new generation from snobbery and flunkeyism.

In Barrie's play "The Admirable Crichton," the butler in the yacht becomes king of the island when the yacht is wrecked. There is a vague feeling in most circles that in close contact with natural surroundings the division of men and women, and still more of boys and girls, into social classes, will not "work." On the frontier, as pioneers, all men and women are equals; and there is at least a trace of that feeling in the Scout movement. Again, Boy Scouts and Girl Guides are to be found in almost all countries, and there is an annual international camp for Scouts. This is another sign of the modern world, growing in the midst of the old divisions and suspicions. I have some friends in a group of Scottish Girl Guides who have visited, as a group, both Denmark and Poland, and have welcomed Danish Girl Guides to Scotland.

It is not implied in the argument so far used, that the Scouts and Guides are admirable because they pursue "education" in their spare time! We are discussing the leisure of children; and their leisure should not be exhausted by efforts to improve them. Indeed it would be best for children to be left to themselves in leisure. What is good in the Scouts and Guides movement is the children's own enjoyment, obtained in their own way; for new forms of friendship are being discovered by these boys and girls in the shared adventure of a return to simpler conditions.

But there are dangers in the modern methods of organizing the leisure of children. Are we not organizing too much? The play of children depends upon space to play in and opportunities for play; and there is a very great need for increasing such opportunities for the majority of children. Poverty or narrow circumstances are far more cramping to children than to adults; and in generation after generation, we are cramping by our economic system the natural movements of the majority of children in all civilized countries. So far, then, as organization is necessary for the provision of opportunities for play, no harm is done. On the other hand, ever since the psychologists and the schoolmasters discovered some value in play, there has been a tendency to organize play too much. Small boys made up adventures and games for themselves long before there was any Scout Movement. Indeed

Lord Baden Powell has said that the Scout movement itself was a spontaneous creation of thousands of small boys and some small girls too. When he had published "Scouting for Boys," little groups of children took up his idea for themselves; and out of that grew the present system. The question is whether some of the organizers of the leisure of children do not nowadays organize too much—and worse still whether they do not use the opportunity unfairly and unwisely for preaching at children. Uniforms and regulations and marching in groups may destroy spontaneity in the play of children and make the world of thirty years hence a world without free laughter.

Whether these movements are progressive or obstructive, it is worth while to consider the general effect of all this upon "the mind of the time" in the children of to-day. Clearly, the new generation will value leisure more highly. Owing to movies and public playgrounds and scouting, thousands of children have had more enjoyment out of leisure than was possible for similar children forty or fifty years ago. The further effect we cannot yet estimate; but certainly we are not repeating the old tradition in the complete molding of a new generation by adults. The new generation is given some opportunity to find its own way;

and it seems probable that its way will not lead them back to where we stand.

Another general effect of recent changes is this. In such uses of leisure as Scouts and Guides enjoy, and even in the movies, some defects of the traditional education are being amended. It is most regrettable that children should still have to "do" geography and history and arithmetic—a meaningless collection of separate subjects, which are the results of dissecting the real world into abstractions. Some teachers do not seem to see that any "subject" taken by itself is a mere ghost of real things; and so the world of childhood is taken apart in the school-room and for many children never put together again. Indeed there are even university students who do not seem to see that an actual man is a more important fact than any "laws" or facts of economics or politics. But the Scouts and the Guides put the world together again in their play; for when you think, not of geography, but of the lie of the land, not of arithmetic, but of the height of the bush—then you may begin to understand what the stuff they talk in schools is all about. Most people have to use their leisure to give a meaning to their work; and children are like the rest of us. Two small boys I know, when they were about ten and twelve years old, made a railway on a shelf that ran round the walls of a room. There was a harbor at one end, where the insides of an old kitchen clock worked a lighthouse which "blinked" as the clock ticked; and there was a frontier where customs officials held up trains. These boys learnt more about the world from their own railway than they learnt from "subjects" at school, because they were putting the world together, not taking it apart. Similarly in scouting boys and girls put the world together for themselves.

Some general conclusions can be made about the change of the attitude toward boys and girls in society. We in the modern world are much more conscious of the importance of childhood than our forefathers were; and perhaps we are more uncertain than they were that we know what to do about it. The changing conditions of modern life —motors instead of horses, movies for spare time, better food and lighter clothing, have been, in the main, for the advantage of children; for children are in happier circumstances if their elders have greater health and vitality and they share in that increase of vitality themselves. One family differs greatly from another; but in general, the larger the family income, the more the children have been in all ages allowed to be egoists; and the smaller the income, the greater the tendency toward swamping all individuality in herd mentality. These are extremes. In less abusive terms—children of poor parents play together more readily and understand one another better, whereas the children of the rich have a greater chance of developing their individual abilities. These, however, are not modern aspects of the situation. They are as ancient as Babylon. But there is no reason why any community should be divided into egoists and members of a herd. What is new is the attempt, here and there being made, to overcome in childhood the division of society into segregate classes as a result of different rates of income. In Germany the common school was intended, after the Revolution of 1918, to bring together all the German children; but the scheme does not appear to have been adopted throughout the republic. In Great Britain no such attempt has been made in the school system, although the Scout movement tends toward social equality. School-fellows are generally playfellows; and in their play children make their friends. The ancient customs of segregation of class from class affects British society from childhood. Parents are more "particular," as we say, about the children with whom their children play than about those with whom they go to school. From the very earliest years the child of the doctor is not supposed to play with the child of the carpenter; and indeed in some towns the child of the railway guard may be separated from the child of the engine cleaner. The more powerful taboos operative in the playtime of children have hardly been affected at all by the changed conditions of the past fifty years. The caste structure of British society is still maintained by the play of children.

The spread of education, however, and the extension of the education of those with low incomes to later years, is destroying the cruder contrasts between members of different social classes. Even poor children are becoming accustomed to play otherwise than in the streets. The "leveling up" of social conditions which has affected adults in the past fifty years has also affected children. The days of the child chimney-sweeper are gone. The weight of incapacity—due to neglect, malnutrition, and gutters to play in, is less burdensome for thousands of children now; and children of poor parents therefore may have a better chance of "standing up" to others, as equals, now that they are better fed, better clothed, better housed. The low vitality of the children in slums still continues, for we have not modernized the city area; but there are many more healthy and vigorous children in poor homes now than there were fifty years ago. Again, the opportunities for play or for the use of leisure are much more equally distributed; for the public parks and the movies are available for those children whose families have low incomes. The radio also is the same for children in different economic classes. And the result is probably a greater similarity of outlook between the children of this generation in all sorts of homes. The evidence is to be found in a consideration of what the doctor's child and the banker's and the dustman's and the railwayman's think and do in spare time; for they think and act in ways that are more similar than their parents' ways were, thirty or forty years ago. The tendency of the modern world is toward social equality; the modernization of the playtime of children makes children of all families more alike in outlook and attitude.

We are in a difficult stage of civilization. The standards of the Middle Ages, which still dominate social custom, are not quite applicable. The landowner's child, the doctor's, the grocer's, the railwayman's, the docker's and the coal-miner's are supposed to be neatly arranged in a gradation of classes, while the education, the leisure occupations, and the entertainments of the new generation are confusing the grades. But strong resistance is maintained against that tendency. It is amusing to watch children trying to acquire the correct attitude toward other children whose parents have different rates of income. The child sometimes makes mistakes, because he misunderstands his parents' criterion of respectability or gentility; but snobbery and flunkeyism are produced by gentle pressure. To be seen playing with the wrong sort of child is soon perceived by any child to be a most serious misdemeanor. By fifteen, most British children have acquired the traditional disdain for other children who are supposed to be in a "lower" class.

The natural tendency will not necessarily be more powerful than the deliberate resistance to it, even if a greater number than at present are willing that the playtime of their own children should promote social equality. But the world of 1950 may very well be divided much more deeply than our world, precisely because the traditional division of classes in accordance with income will correspond to actual conditions even less than it does now, after another twenty years of the new uses of leisure. Ignorance of any alternative tends to preserve acquiescence in a tradition. But knowledge of the advantages due to economic privileges, may disturb the acquiescence of those who do not share such privileges. What is at issue now, therefore, in the habits and attitudes of children, is division or coöperation between the men and women of fifty years hence. The divisions, if there are to be divisions, will cut deeper than political disagreement. Coöperation, if there is to be coöperation across the frontier of inequal incomes or national rivalry, will have been secured by the uses of leisure among the children of to-day. But it will hardly be possible much longer to live among tendencies toward social equality and to maintain, without any deep resentment, the traditional castes. Conscious policy in such organizations as that of the Scouts will have to be directed more definitely so as to support or to transform traditional divisions. At present the leaders of such movements, at any rate in Great Britain, have developed very thoroughly the old British habit of "dodging the issue"—which is called "compromise." But are the Scouts and Guides of to-day to make men and women of tomorrow divided into "upper" and "lower" classes or are they to learn equality? Are they to be "national" in opposition to other nations or to subordinate "the flag" quite definitely to a wider loyalty? The answer to such questions will be forced upon the world by circumstances. They cannot be put aside much longer. And as for the less consciously directed influences of custom in playtime, they too may produce a situation in which it will be no longer possible to maintain both medieval caste and modern equality—as we do now—in a precarious adjustment of incompatible ideas and habits.

of youth," because a new generation comes into existence not at the birth of the body but at the birth of the soul, in adolescence; and every new generation finds itself somewhat cramped by the structure of social custom and belief, which is already established. Every social system practises abortion, if it does injury to adolescence. Some are brought forth too soon; and their spirits faint and die in the grind or the uncertainty of industrial occupations. There are millions of bodies walking about without souls in them because their youthful dreams were destroyed. But if by any chance at adolescence the soul survives and is strong, there is a "revolt of youth." This revolt is quite natural; but it is so weak in our primitive civilization and, when it occurs, it seems so strange, that there actually are old gentlemen who jump out of their skins, if any one younger than they are, doubts the value of their experience. Experience, as Oscar Wilde said, is the long name we all give to our own mistakes; and in that sense there is no doubt of the experience of the old. History is a record of mistakes. We should learn from history never to let history repeat itself. But that is what youth has always tried to do; and it has usually failed.

However, here we are in 1932, and some of us are still between fifteen and twenty-five. The problem is this. Adolescence has many times occurred in many different societies and civilizations, but now adolescence is occurring in a world of movies and motor-cars and radio. And in that world the majority, who are older, still belong to a world in which such things were strange and new; but young men and women to-day have had no experience of a world without movies and motor-cars. Their leisure occupations are quite different from the leisure occupations of their parents, when they were young. They inhabit a larger and more varied world. Again, the new world of mechanisms is only the outer sign of a new world of thought or mental attitudes. Films and motor-cars are modern knowledge and modern desires in their simplest or crudest material form. Clearly the new world of modern thought is not so widespread as the use of new mechanisms; for very few are aware of the new forms of music and painting and literature, the new scientific outlook, and the new kinds of philosophy. And yet young people generally have a feeling of freedom and adventure which corresponds in the lives of ordinary folk to the movement of the new sciences and the new arts in the world at large. Young people who are affected by the modern world feel much less bound than their parents were by the traditional ortho-

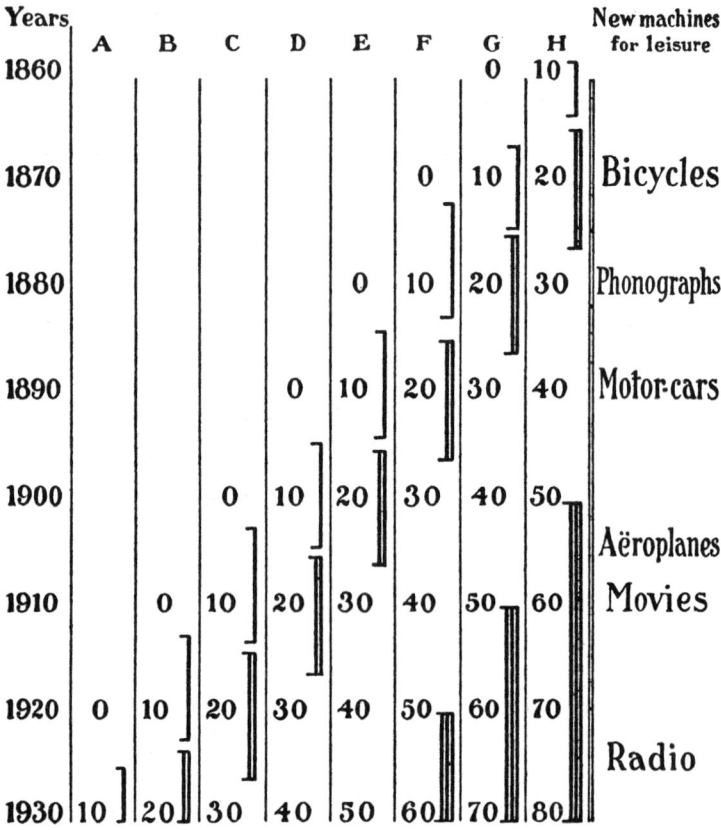

SUGGESTIONS DRAWN FROM TABLE

1. In 1930, those in control of public affairs in politics, industry, and education, being between 50 and 70, were in *old age* during the great period of change and therefore have been less deeply affected by those changes than those who are younger.

2. These same older men and women were at school *before* the new education began; and many of the oldest have had very inadequate education.

3. Those who are now "mature," between 25 and 50, received education *before* the period of war and revolution but in the period when the first steps were being made in the new education.

4. Only those under 20 have come into a world in which movies and radio were already commonplace; for all others these inventions have to be "digested" into a mental structure formed without their influence.

5. The opinions of people of each age as to the new uses of leisure depend upon what their age was when the new uses first became common. People of 80 probably feel that bicycles go too fast. People of over 50 are worried about movies.

6. New machines for leisure. This column shows the dates at which each of the machines first came into general use—not the dates of invention.

7. The change from the primitive "scarcity" to modern "plenty" in the economic situation occurred somewhere between 1860 and 1930. The mental change which would be an adjustment to this new situation has not yet occurred; but the beginning is perhaps to be traced in the new attitude toward leisure.

8. The proportion of the population, in any country, of different age at different dates makes a great difference to the uses of leisure. In Great Britain the percentage of those under 15 went down from 37% in 1891 to 29% in 1921. Also countries differ in the proportion of the youthful. In England and Wales in 1921 there were 185 boys and 184 girls under 19 per 1,000 living; in the United States in 1920 the proportion was 205 boys and 203 girls.

doxies and the traditional standards of what ought to be done. But this does not imply, as some think, that they do not feel bound at all; for the traditional beliefs and customs are not the only ones possible.

The universal peculiarities of youth have been admirably studied in Stanley Hall's great work on "Adolescence": and it would take too long to summarize what is now known about the physical and psychological changes which precede adult manhood or womanhood. The difficulties which are referred to when there is a discussion of "the revolt of youth" nowadays, are due to the social and intellectual conditions within which these universal changes are occurring. That is why we hear so much about "sex appeal" in the films, and, at least in America, about coeducation in universities, and about freer companionship between young men and women. The old interests and impulses are still powerful; but they are "in play" in a world which is different from that of the nineteenth century. The first question, therefore, is how these interests and impulses actually do find outlets or satisfactions to-day.

Quite apart from any organized movement, there is a desire among the youthful to escape from the home surroundings of their childhood. This may be partly due to the feeling that parents and relatives never recognize when a child ceases to be a child. Indeed it requires a vigorous imagination in parents to see the "new person" who was once, as a child, dependent upon them; and many parents and relatives continue to command or advise long after they should have learnt to treat the younger generation as equals. Teachers suffer from the same "delayed perception"; they continue to adopt a superior air long after the former pupil has become a man or woman. In very simple societies, as in parts of China and India to-day, the younger generation never escapes from the direction of the older until the older dies. That is called the family system. We have been a long time in Europe in escaping from it; but in the modern world, when a child becomes a man or woman, the relationship of dependence ceases. If any one older attempts to retain control over the now adult person, the friction or mutual irritation occurs which many of us have observed in our own circles. But the actual strain or struggle is usually felt most acutely in adolescence; because at that time the person who was lately a child, often without knowing what is happening, feels the conflict within, which is the new struggling to be born out of the old. In the United States unique circumstances have made the struggle more acute; for millions of young folk there, who have been to school, have immigrant parents who retain the old superstitions, and may not even speak English. The distinction between the outlooks of the two generations there is obvious. But even in Great Britain, the world into which the new generation has been introduced, both in their schooling and in the occupations of their leisure, is so different from what their parents' world was when they were young, that the distinction between the attitudes of the two generations is obvious here also. In France it is less so. In Germany and Central Europe more so. And in general, what we call the modern world is a social situation in which the division between the generations is greater than it was hitherto. This shows itself in the tendency to "leave home" after adolescence, but still more in the tendency to seek companionship outside the family. The relation between the older generation and the youthful in the modern world, is much less one of dependence than it has usually been in the past. The authority of tradition—that is to say, of grandmothers and grandfathers, is less powerful. This is due, not only to present conditions in the use of leisure, but also to the peculiarity of the period in which those who are now between fifteen and twenty-five were educated—a period of great social uncertainty. No wonder, then, that tradition is weak among the youth in all European countries. But we must not assume that a tradition which led to the war was so wonderfully good that weakening it must be bad.

Again, city areas, within which great numbers of the younger generation are living and have lived throughout childhood, cause, in reaction against them, an appetite for Nature in hills and woods and sea and clouds. That is the source of "rambling" or "hiking." But consider now the same movement from the point of view of the child who is becoming a man. Every one knows the tendency of adolescence to be moved by the moon; poets, who are often in delayed adolescence, "work" the moon very hard. But indeed all natural sights and sounds give a certain relief to adolescents; and the conditions of modern city life seem to act as a repression from which relief is sought. It is well known that "Nature," as we think of it, is a discovery of city dwellers. The poets of the coffee-houses and not the shepherds, wrote what is called "pastoral poetry." Indeed what earlier ages thought objectionable in nature—rocks and mountains and stones—have been admired only since we acquired the psychological perspective—the "distance" by which we can see them better from the securities of the city. You cannot see "Nature" if you are too close up to it. But the city dweller during adolescence tends to revive the earlier contacts of the human race, now made conscious and desirable; and with that goes the modern attitude toward material things. The youth of the modern world have not that fear of bodily experience which grew out of the ignorance of their forefathers. It would be going too far to say that the youthful have a new philosophy; but certainly they have a new attitude. There is much less fear: and they are much less easily frightened. Therefore the morality which depended upon the threat of evil consequences is less effectual than it used to be; the belief in "hell" has evaporated even in the churches and there is too much distrust of the authority of the past for the youthful to be controlled by fear of what they are told their actions will bring upon them. As for the traditional fear of natural impulse, the new generation begins to see that no bodily appetite or function is unholy or unclean, that beauty and health are not temptations or dangers. This combines with a new attitude toward leisure and the enjoyment of leisure; for the new generation does not believe that its leisure is for the sake of its work. Therefore, the more leisure, the better; and the more one can enjoy leisure, the better. The younger generation does not lack energy; but it feels that its energy ought not to be expended mainly in the effort to obtain a bare existence.

By far the most striking change however in the attitude of the youthful is in their treatment of companionship with persons of the opposite sex. The evidence of change is inadequate, because what happens in any one's experience of the people among whom he lives may not be in the least typical. I am therefore not asserting that there is a general or widespread change: I am in fact only asking whether you have observed any change among the youthful of your acquaintance. I do not mean to ask whether they are better or worse. Let us leave that problem undiscussed. We want to discover first in what respects, if any, they are different from what those were, who were youthful about thirty or forty years ago, in their manners and customs, or in their attitude toward persons of an opposite sex. It must be remembered that until women had the same sort of education as men, there could hardly be intelligent companionship between the sexes; and while the leisure occupations of men separated them from women, no common outlook could be formed. Now girls have been receiving education for about a generation and companionship of young men and women is quite common in visiting movies, in "rambling" or "hiking" and in some games; and the radio is just as much available for women as for men. The result seems to be less "strangeness" dividing or attracting the two sexes in adolescence; for the relationship is much more like the companionship of equals, each of whom knows more about the other than their parents did twenty years ago. The attitude of each is more frankly experimental; and plain speaking is commoner than it used to be. Romance has gained in depth by refusing to avert its eyes from reality.

Two very different attitudes are adopted toward these changes in attitude of modern youth. Some say that the weakening of tradition in the younger generation is bad and should be counteracted by organization or influence. They say that adolescence is a period for guidance or direction given by those who have already passed through it; that the store of moral knowledge already acquired, like our knowledge of arithmetic, is adequate to provide principles of guidance; that leisure is an opportunity for more than mere enjoyment, or for going to church instead of going for country walks.

Others, on the contrary, welcome the weakening of tradition, because so many of the evils from which we now suffer are inherited. Such people say that poverty and war and the subjection of women have not been destroyed by quoting authorities—have indeed been maintained by such quotation. It is argued that not all the rules of the past are applicable to conditions unimagined in the past; and even if the past did in fact discover some truth, the faculty for discovery has not been exhausted. It is not a case of old standards as against no standards, but of accepting old standards as against the discovery of new standards. Those who welcome the modern revolt of youth say that the past must make its case; for it cannot be assumed that it is wiser than the younger generation.

So far the argument has implied that the revolt of youth is the accidental result of the use of new opportunities in leisure. But there is also a conscious and deliberate organization of youth, especially for the use of leisure in the discussion or the control of public affairs. The force, in the spirit of the youth of to-day, is more fluid, more amenable to influence than ever before; and a deliberate effort is being made to direct this force, in various forms of Youth Movement. The distinction between all such movements and the youth organizations of earlier times, lies in this—that all genuine Youth

Movements are *spontaneous*. They are not to be confounded with clubs for improving youth, nor with associations organized by older people for capturing the new generation for some party. There is a spontaneous and original impulse toward association among younger men and women. In its cruder expressions it can be seen in the "gangs" formed in city streets by boys with energy to spare. Such gangs have all the characteristics of primitive human "packs." They have secret signs, a language of their own, often an "enemy" to oppose, and leaders who embody the ideal of the gang member. The same type of association is to be found among girls, but generally not so well developed. All this, however, is old. What is new within the past fifty years is the spontaneous large-scale organization of youth for the expression of what is felt to be a new attitude toward life and the world. When groups of young men and women are spontaneously organized for such a purpose, we speak of a Youth Movement; and the most famous and perhaps the most important Youth Movement is in Germany. It began before the war, about 1900, with a "return to nature." It was a revolt against the deadening influences of city life in the industrial era; and its moving spirits revived the old German Romanticism. They sang the old German folk-songs and danced the traditional dances of the country-side. They were in revolt against industrial militaristic authoritarian Germany but not against the older Germany, which as in many revolts, was falsely imagined to have been all freedom and gaiety. The war came; and the break between the generations was all the greater because so many of the younger men were killed. After the war, the German Youth Movement attempted to initiate a new world without war and oppression. But the revival of older controversies in politics and religion caused a division of the youth into the old camps; and now there are youth movements in all camps, but whether all the youth will be absorbed into the old camps or the old camps will be transformed by the youth remains to be seen.

In many other countries where social changes have been drastic, the youth have played a new part. Student movements have been the chief supports of "nationalism" in Egypt and India and China; students have organized revolution in Spain. There are less powerful but no less significant student groups in South America. In Russia and in Italy youth groups are partly spontaneous, partly created in support of Communism and Fascism. In Great Britain the National Union of Students has attempted to express the attitude of the new generation on public affairs; and the N.U.S. is connected with similar organizations abroad through the International Confederation of Students.

All this indicates an important social change of the past thirty years. The younger generation is not merely affected by new uses of leisure for entertainment; it is deliberately using some of its leisure for affecting public policy. Girls as well as young men are in this movement; and in some countries, such as China and Turkey and India, the action taken by girl students is more startling because the traditional position of women has been so different. It is true that students cease to be students and youths become adults; but while they are students and youths, these younger folk are criticizing the established order and asking very pointed questions, which the statesmen and politicians and industrial leaders of the world do not always answer to the satisfaction of the younger generation. The proportion of fools in every generation is about the same; and therefore the youthful as a whole are not any wiser than the aged. They can be taken in by the same old game. But a social change is implied in the greater tendency of the youthful to ask pointed questions about fundamental issues and the greater disinclination to accept the traditional answers.

There is, in practice, some disagreement about the attitude which should be adopted toward the spontaneous desire of youth to play its own part in public affairs. Some say that the youth should be "organized": and the result of such organization is not a youth movement but different and even opposed groups—the Young Conservatives, the Young Liberals, the Young "Labor" group, the Young Catholics, and the Young Protestants. Thus the leisure of youth is actually used in order to train recruits for the old armies. The "revolt of youth" against authority is thus neutralized by being directed into the traditional hostilities; and the most popular of all the traditional hostilities is that of "nationalism." The violent emotions of adolescence and especially of delayed adolescence, are used to reinforce an obsolete policy of division between the peoples of the world. The leisure of the younger generation is organized with a view to the maintenance of a fantastic "national" tradition—if not in actual military training, at least in enthusiasm for an old cause.

On the other hand, an entirely different attitude toward Youth Movements is adopted by the modern mind. This attitude implies that the youth of to-day is seeking three new things, first a finer skill in the discovery of personality, secondly a progressive in place of a static morality, and thirdly a radical reëxamination of social, religious, political, and economic institutions. Let me try to explain this point of view. First, as to the discovery of personality, it must be assumed that any man or woman worth knowing at all has more "inside" than appears at first sight. Indeed what there is "in" a man or a woman may not come into play except under the influence of another person. But the effect of one person upon another may be surprising to both. All contact or conversation, therefore, is a voyage of discovery; you cannot tell what you will find; and besides, what you find may not have been there at all until you set to work to find it. Now modern conditions seem to have increased the ease and directness with which men and women can meet. Naturally new problems of morality as well as of manners may arise; but the skill in the discovery of personality and in the development of one's own capacities through intimate intercourse may be improved by the fresh and vigorous impulses of youth. Confidence in the value of free and generous intercourse is not shaken, if some of the youthful are fools; for civilized life in society is not based upon the control of fools or criminals, but upon the normal tendency of human beings toward kindliness and friendship. The assumption is that if men and women learn to know one another better, they will usually find what is worth knowing. From this point of view, the obsolescence of moral control by the use of fear, which has been referred to above, leaves the field open for positive and progressive standards. For example, the threat of evil consequences following certain actions is less effectual than an indication of the delight or vitality which would follow other actions. In the intercourse between the sexes, in particular, the range and fullness of a civilized experience are hardly yet known. The momentary and transitory impulse, with which youth is familiar, is not misleading, unless it is given a trivial satisfaction. But to repress an impulse often drives it into trivial courses, whereas to expect more from it, gives it a larger place in the whole of life. One may very well question an impulse. There are illusions of mental life and of emotion, as there are illusions of the eye; and it is not true that we know the "self" better than we know chairs or tables. Most people and indeed also most scientific psychologists are subject to illusions about the "self." But what is unknown is not to be feared; it is the subject-matter for experiment and discovery. The guiding hypothesis for such experiment is that there is more in any person and in any situation than "meets the eye"—that, in fact, only artistic skill can "bring out" what it is right to do in any circumstances. But this implies a progressive, in place of a static morality.

By static morality is meant the acceptance of certain standards, prohibitions, taboos, or admirations, derived from an established tradition. Such a morality involves an authoritarian view of the teaching of morality; that is to say, it assumes that what is right is already known and that nothing more is needed but preaching it. In science and in the fine arts, however, we no longer accept authoritarian teaching; nor do we suppose that any age has reached final conclusions. Why then should it be supposed that, in the art of life which is morality, we or our grandfathers have reached final conclusions? No one supposes that we may discover that it is right to kill or to tell lies, after having questioned taboos against these acts. It is not implied that the past was wrong: it is argued only that the knowledge of personality and of the intercourse between persons in the past was very limited. How to make love, how to pass through adolescence best, how to meet and to part from others

—all these problems have not yet begun to be explored. And modern youth does not believe that there are ready-made rules as to how best two persons of opposite sexes may interact upon one another, or how government or industry ought to be organized. If, then, one supposes that in morality, as in science or art, experiment is the basis of knowledge and skill, and also that knowledge and skill in morality can improve, then one's morality is progressive and not static. The past, then, may contain interesting suggestions but neither final rules nor models. What simpler ages condemned as bad, may have been thought bad only because of ignorance; for, especially in the relation between the sexes, all traditional morality assumes, for example, the inferiority of women and therefore has no evidence at all about the relationship of men and women who are equals. Further, traditional morality over-estimated the importance and misinterpreted the place of the sexual impulse. We now know more psychology. It is impossible, therefore, to accept the conclusions of the past on a subject on which it was in the dark.

Again, the attitude of modern youth with regard to the inherited political and economic institutions is more radical than ever before. Why should the new generation accept the conditions under which their forefathers sought to secure political order or food and clothing? Education should produce, not new toilers in the old mill, but men and women too good for the shabby gentilities and ill-rewarded labors of existing society. In all former ages the old and the dead have dominated the world; for stability and security have been thought better than risk and experiment. Now perhaps youth can contribute. The result would be a society much more alive and vigorous in all its human relationships. Such is the attitude implied in the unconscious restlessness of the youth of today, which is called the revolt of youth, and such also is the deliberate policy of youth groups which seek to direct the generous impulses of adolescence towards the establishment of a new community.

XI

CIVILIZATION AND THE LEISURED CLASS

WE may now discuss the ideals consciously or unconsciously implied in recent changes in the use of leisure. Extended leisure among those who work for a living has been shown to involve a tendency toward social equality; and the deliberate use of the new leisure in social movements has, in the main, reinforced that tendency. The question now is whether or not a new form of social structure is implied, if recent tendencies become dominant. The relations between men, women, and children in any community are at least partly governed by those emotional conceptions of what is desirable, which are called ideals. Certain kinds of character, of outlook or activity, of intercourse or individuality are regarded as worth working for; and even if the majority have no clear conception of what they desire, a common standard, "in the air" in social life, has influence upon all. It was implied or assumed, for example, in the Middle Ages, that a saint removed from the world was the best type of human character; and in the eighteenth century it was implied that only a few could have the opportunities in leisure for developing the finest type of civilized life. What corresponding ideals are operative in the modern world?

The displacement of the leisured class as the preservers and promoters of culture is the most significant of all the changes in our traditional social system, which are the results of the new uses of leisure. The characteristics of these new uses have been described in the preceding chapters. The great majority—who have to work for a living in factories, shops, and offices—have *more spare time* and *more energy* to spend in their spare time, than their grandparents had. Also they have had, since about 1890 or 1900, a new and much more interesting kind of education in the schools, which has given them new abilities to use in spare time. For example, they can read more easily than their grandparents could; they know more about the world outside their homes; and they are also healthier and stronger. By a succession of accidents of discovery and invention, new uses of spare time have come in, which are available for those with small incomes and even a little spare time. The moving picture, the radio, the phonograph, and the motor-car are democratic in the sense that great numbers of people can use them; whereas the opera or the theater, the concert, and the horse-carriage were available only for a few.

Obviously, all this has changed the relationship between what used to be called "the leisured class" and the rest of the community. In all former civilizations a "leisured class" has been the support of public policy, of social culture, and of the finest development of civilization in the arts and the sciences. The leisure of this "leisured class" was valuable, not merely for themselves, but for the whole of the community to which they belonged and to the world—to us, in fact, who look back to the achievements of Athens and Florence and eighteenth-century France. But now at last the extension of leisure among those who work for a living and the new uses of their leisure have completely changed the position of a leisured class.

It is possible to argue that civilization still depends upon the existence and activity of a "leisured class"; and indeed, that point of view has been expressed in a recent book on civilization.[1] I shall not argue about ancient history. It may not have

---

[1] Clive Bell, "Civilization" p. 205—"Civilization requires the existence of a leisured class, and a leisured class requires the existence of slaves—of people, I mean, who give some part of their surplus time and energy to the support of others." This is the best example of an obsolete view of the "leisured class"; but the same view is often expressed in the London "Times," both in its correspondence columns and in its editorial pages.

been possible for a few thousand men in ancient Athens to work out the beginnings of democracy in public affairs, or to support the arts and sciences, without using slaves and women as instruments for their "good life." It may not have been possible for King Louis XIV to build the Palace of Versailles without the forced labor of the thousands who now lie buried in its neighborhood. But I am not concerned with them. I am talking of 1932, in Europe and America. And here too, it is contended by some that a "leisured class" is essential for the proper consideration of public policy, and for the support of the sciences and the arts. The leisured class thus fulfils a function in the community, and is not a mere ornament. No one, I suppose, would claim that a leisured class actually produces the sciences or the arts or the dominant conceptions of public policy. The argument is that the leisured class is necessary to provide an "atmosphere" within which these may flourish; or that leisure produces civilization only when it is the secure possession of a class of men and women who are not obliged to work for a living. It is assumed in this view that leisure is not merely for the entertainment of those who have it; but that such persons do and should use some of their leisure for the consideration of public affairs. It is also assumed that the *free* enjoyment of any activities one likes, is an essential part of civilized life. What is added, is that, some men and women in any civilized community must be distinguishable from others as belonging to a "leisured class." That is the traditional view.

On the other hand, a "modern" view of leisure implies that we are passing into an entirely new kind of civilization in which a "leisured class" will have no function at all to perform. Leisure, then, will not be peculiar to a "class" or group within the community, but will be shared in all its uses by every member of the community. This view is supported by a study of the change which has occurred in the common attitude toward the leisure of those who work for a living. At one time—not very long ago—spare time was regarded as an unimportant interval in what was considered to be characteristic of their lives—namely work. That kind of leisure was supposed to have its excuse or justification in its utility for the purposes of work. It was regarded as a misuse of that leisure if it were spent in doing anything that made a man or woman less able to work; and therefore such leisure and its uses were "slavish," in the sense that they existed for the sake of something different—"production" or "service" or what not. It was in fact slave's leisure—not the leisure which the Greek philosophers believed to be the seed-patch of civilization. Some little flowers were grown in it; but they were like the poor flowers that one sees sometimes in the midst of factory buildings. These nineteenth-century flowers were the hymns of those who bore most of the burdens and shared little of the benefits of oligarchic industrialism; they were the poems of Mrs. Hemans —poems to be read in the intervals of the more serious business of life—elegant poems, but not such as would drive a man mad or prevent his going back to work. Even the leisure of Sunday was often so used as to make Monday's work a relief; for those whose whole lives were supposed to be given meaning or value only by their work, who were called the "working class," in contrast to the "leisured class." Holidays, which used to be holy days, then became in England "bank" holidays, as if what was most important about them was that the banks were shut.

About fifty years ago, however, a new current set in. The leisure of bankers and butchers and doctors and dustmen—all of whom had to work for a living —came to be more and more filled by new entertainments and enjoyments. The social and economic causes of this, as it was suggested in an earlier chapter, were increased productive power, stable or decreasing populations, decrease of the number of dependents on each family income and increase of spare money for "luxuries." But education and better diet also had their effects; and the result was that the leisure of those who had to work began to be valued for its own sake. Men and women enjoyed what they had in leisure, not because it made them work better, but because it gave them life outside of work. And gradually even the preachers began to discover that there was something valuable in enjoyment. It is still the habit of preachers to attack gambling or drinking, without allowing for the enjoyment in them which is good, because there is still a suspicion that enjoying yourself is sinful. Obviously there are objectionable ways of enjoying yourself; but there are also most objectionable ways of working for a living; and if one cannot condemn all work because some is slavish, one should not be suspicious of all enjoyment because some is mistaken. It is remarkable, in any case, that better means of enjoyment have been discovered without the aid of preachers. Reformers a century ago, for example, used to urge those whom they called "the workers" to drink less gin; but the movies—an alternative form of enjoyment—have done more than the advocates of temperance to lessen the amount of drunkenness. The uses of leisure have become more civilized than they were, owing to the discovery of better means of enjoyment, but such means can be discovered only when enjoyment itself is assumed to be desirable. Not merely a momentary relief from work but a life outside the world of work was discovered by the majority in the use of the new opportunities. It is now beginning to be felt that the leisure of those who work can be valuable for the control of public policy, for the discovery of undeveloped capacities in one's self, for the creation of a new world to be enjoyed here and now. Thus the worker's leisure may become the source of a high civilization and not merely, as in old days, the leisure of the "leisured class." Leisure still remains the seed-plot of civilization, but this leisure need no longer be the possession of a separate social class. The social function performed by a leisured class in the past can now be performed by those who have to work for a living. They can contribute the consideration of public affairs, the free experiment in new kinds of activity and whatever comes out of enjoying yourself without any other purpose than the enjoyment. Such is the modern view.

The argument, however, is not concluded at this point; for the traditionalist may return to the attack. He will say that it is impossible to discover what may happen, but that in fact what does happen does not show that more extended leisure, fuller of new uses, improves civilized life. He will contend that the modernist confuses quantity with quality; that it does not matter, as a test of civilization, how many have leisure nor how many hours of it they have, nor how many film or radio entertainments they may enjoy. What matters is the quality of personality and the tone of social intercourse, which is the result. But—so it is argued—the new leisure and its new uses have not produced anything as fine as was produced in the past. The traditionalist in this mood and especially the French traditionalist tends to say at this point— "Look at America! There is mechanized superficiality, mistaken by its victims for civilized life!" From this, says the traditionalist, we are saved by a leisured class. All your movies, he says, are only recent versions of the popular entertainments at medieval fairs—good enough for "spare time" but not for true leisure.

What can the modernist reply to the traditionalist? First, he will reply that the traditionalist underestimates the depth of the social change which has taken place; something more has happened in the past fifty years than happened when the middle ages passed into the eighteenth century. One sign of this new change is education—not merely in schools, but through cheap books and newspapers, films, and radio. Coal-miners and railwaymen and shopkeepers and women who manage households on small incomes can now read and listen to music and see strange lands and peoples and even do some calculation, in ways that used to be possible only for a few clerks or secretaries in older civilizations. Secondly, great numbers of them think keenly on public affairs and already have power to influence public affairs. Thirdly, the modernist will say that the tendency in the new uses of leisure is to destroy the sense of inferiority and superiority—or at any rate to destroy the former. Those who assume that they are in an "upper" class continue to assume it long after others, in what used to be regarded as a "lower" class, cease to feel inferior. But ceasing to feel inferior may be a result of education or of new opportunities in the use of leisure or of new ways of living or of new kinds of occupation. Social changes of outlook and attitude sometimes precede economic and political changes. A man may feel himself by no means "inferior" long before he ceases to depend upon another man for his livelihood or his civil liberties. And what a man feels about himself may cause explosions. Feelings, pent up or unrealized in a social system, tend to increase their pressure, as steam will increase in pressure when there is no safety-valve. And the feeling of one man that he is not "inferior" combines with the similar feeling of another. The steam under pressure in many minds is a force within the whole of a social system; the explosion may be so widespread as to destroy the system itself. That is what happened when a Court aristocracy was challenged by the so-called *bourgeois* in the French Revolution. Quite apart from the resentment against political privilege, there was a "social" pressure from the middle classes against the superior airs of those who had the traditional culture. To these latter, of course, it seemed like an invasion of barbarism from below that the courtiers and their ladies, who knew drawing-room rituals, should not be treated as superior by lawyers and doctors who were "lower" classes. So Amiel—a survivor of antiquity, writes of democracy that its coming destroys all good manners and the graces of life.[2] If all the manners you know are drawing-room manners, then you cannot see that the manners of streets and shops become better, not worse, in proportion as there is an approach to equal status in the relationship of men. What happens in drawing-rooms may be worse; but that is not so important as the change

---

[2] "Le prodigieux déluge démocratique. . . . Il faut se résigner à ce qu'il commence par tout enlaidir et par tout vulgariser, de même que l'intrusion soudaine de la rue dans le salon submerge la bonne société et réduit au silence les gens comme il faut." Amiel's Journal.

outside. From such evidence the modernist concludes that the function performed in former civilizations by a "leisured class" can now be performed without the existence of such a class; that, in fact, leisure as the basis for civilization at its best is not, in modern conditions, the privilege of a class. And this implies that the leisure of those who work is not, in fact, merely a rest from work, but a source of new life in a new sphere. The modernist may indeed go further if with Veblen, for example, in his "Theory of the Leisure Class" he feels inclined to criticize adversely the customs and beliefs of leisured classes in any civilization. He may accept the challenge of the traditionalist to "look at America" and reply—"Well! I find it good! And do you, Mr. Traditionalist, regard the life of the French courtier in the old régime or of the Indian prince as 'civilized'?" The courtier enjoyed the public torture of criminals. The Indian prince is blind to the conditions on which his wealth depends. America and democracy are not like that. However, there is no end to this argument. Some believe that civilization is what has already occurred; and others believe that it is what has not yet occurred. The latter are modernists.

In any case, the new attitude toward leisure among those who work has two important effects upon what is commonly thought about social distinctions. In the first place, when those who do the work on which civilization depends have spare time and energy to see the work they do in the whole "setting" of their lives, they see that work is as noble as leisure. The sharp division between work and leisure breaks down when there is no class in a community which can be called a working class, as contrasted with a leisured class, because all men have both leisure and work. Enjoyment then spills over from leisure into work, even if all work is for the sake of leisure. The conception of work for the sake of leisure does not degrade, it elevates the value set upon work, because what is done in leisure is conceived to be real life, which reflects back upon what is done at work. The existence of a leisured class in former civilizations tended to make men believe that work was a curse from which any one who could, should escape. As C. E. Montague wrote: "So powerful is the innate craving for labor that it may take all the massed resources of a great public school and of a famous and ancient University to make a boy believe that real work is a thing to flee from, like want or disease, and that doing it and 'having a good time' are states naturally and inevitably opposed to one another." [3] That is the tradition of a

[3] A writer's notes on his Trade, p. 210. C. E. Montague.

slave civilization, preserved perhaps unconsciously in a "classical" education. But we are now at the beginning of a new age in which a man or a woman will live a whole life, both in work and in leisure, and will not divide time into the objectionable and the insignificant—work you hate to do and leisure you need not do anything with. In the second place, when civilized life at its best is seen to be possible not merely for a leisured class but also in the leisure of those who work, then "social climbing" will be less common. As J. A. Hobson says, in his study called "Towards Social Equality"—"No form of self satisfaction is more definite than the sense of rising from a lower to a higher social status. It is at once a testimonial to personal merit and a triumph over inferiors who were formerly one's equals." He goes on to say that "the condition of England in mid-Victorian times was peculiarly favorable to the stimulation of the social climbing instinct." That condition has not yet changed. It is still generally believed that some one with nothing to do is somehow "superior." But a suspicion of other possibilities is beginning to corrode the complacency of the social climber; and others are watching with hardly concealed amusement the efforts of a leisured class to keep up its confidence by publicity in the illustrated press and the "society" news. H. G. Wells, in his latest book, has remarked that the rich in contemporary society are no longer treated as integral parts of its structure.

> The outward radiation of the mentality and example of the contemporary rich . . . is not even all-powerful in evoking styles and fashions. Its prestige is very great, but not so great relatively as was the prestige of the nobility and gentry of France and England and the small royalties and princes of Germany and Italy in the eighteenth century. . . . The snobbish imitativeness and life at second-hand which formerly prevailed (among the people of middling fortune) are becoming relatively unimportant.[4]

If this is so, then we are passing into a new form of civilization, in which experiments in new ways of living and standards of excellence will not be derived from a segregate social or economic class. Where common folk are free, as in leisure, to make a variety of choices, the standards of what is best will arise from the success of the few who are exceptional in the art of life but are not distinguishable as a separate class.

But we must not go too fast for the evidence. The recent extension of leisure and the many new uses of leisure for those who work, have only just begun to change the traditional social system. It is by no means certain that what has begun will continue.

[4] H. G. Wells, "Work, Wealth, etc.," p. 478, English ed., 1932.

There may be a set-back. Hours of work may be increased, the family incomes of the majority may become smaller—so that fewer uses of leisure will be possible; and we may return to the social situation of the early industrial period. If that happens, it will not be due to natural forces, nor to any mythological "economic laws," but to incompetence in using our new productive powers for social progress; and already the set-back has begun in Germany and the United States and Great Britain.

Let us suppose however that the changes of the past fifty years are continued in the same direction as that so far followed—that leisure is extended for those who work and that the uses of leisure by them will become still more numerous and varied. Only so could the new civilization arise, of which we now see the first shoots. If the best elements of civilized life are to grow out of the leisure, not of a "leisured class," but of those who work for a living—such leisure must be increased. It is assumed that civilized life consists, first, in skill in such ordinary things as cooking and wearing the right clothes and having the right color on the walls. On that skill is based, secondly, the civilization of social intercourse—its graces and its delicacies. And on that again is based the finest flower of civilization—the creation and appreciation of the sciences and the fine arts. But at every stage and all through such a civilized life runs the sense of the community which has its outward expression in the concern with public affairs called "citizenship." All this can come out of the leisure of those who work; but only if that leisure is longer and more widespread than it now is. In spite of recent advances, too many men and women—especially women, are without enough leisure and without enough opportunities for using leisure. Also the schools have not so far given men and women enough skill in the use of such opportunities as they already possess. The greater extension of leisure, therefore, must be accompanied by a change in the system of education, and that change is occurring. The best schools nowadays aim at teaching their pupils how to live, and not merely how to make a living. But we need not wait for a new education before reducing hours of work and decreasing the fatigue incidental to the older forms of work; for the best way of learning how to use leisure is to have more than enough leisure to use.

If therefore the leisure of those who work has not yet produced a higher type of civilization than was produced by the leisure of a leisured class, the reason may be that there is not enough of this new leisure. In any case, the civilization which would arise out of the leisure of those who work would be very different in its finest products from earlier slave civilizations. The standards derived from those earlier civilizations may not be applicable. The forms of art and even the social structure of scientific thought may be very unlike the traditional; and it is conceivable that those who have been most carefully trained in the traditional standards may be the last to recognize the new civilization for what it is. Many times in history, in communities which have undergone far less radical changes than ours, a new form of beauty or truth has been condemned by the cultured as barbaric ugliness or falsity. Regarded, therefore, simply as a field for experiment, the new leisure may reveal not merely new types of fine action or clear thinking, but new standards; and these new standards would apply both to the forms of art and to the characters and relationships of men and women in a new kind of community.

XII

NEW LEISURE MAKES NEW MEN

It is a new kind of fact in history that millions of folk who work for their living should not merely have leisure, but have leisure with energy unexhausted and with many different opportunities for using it. This new kind of leisure never existed, at least on such a scale, fifty years ago. There was indeed "time off"; but most of those who had to work were worn out before they left work. And besides, the number of ways of occupying leisure was much smaller. There was no movie nor radio. A new kind of leisure has come into existence. It is not simply the old leisure of "leisured classes" extended to other people. It is an entirely different kind of leisure.

Let it be granted that this leisure is often misused in modern communities. That is nothing new. Leisure has always been misused. It is romance, not history, to suppose that the majority of those who had leisure in ancient Athens, conversed on philosophy with Socrates or produced poems and sculpture. Again, eighteenth-century "upper classes" had leisure; and it was not less misused than their leisure is misused by modern democracies. Clearly if an educated man is drunk, he may express himself in quotations, whereas the uneducated drunkard is more original; but that does not make the old drunkenness more admirable. Modern conditions are not exceptional in the wasting of leisure; and it is quite impossible to estimate whether leisure is *more* or *less* wasted to-day than it used to be. Therefore it must not be assumed that the defects of movie-going or betting or crowding at public games prove anything against what is sometimes called "democracy." But "two blacks do not make a white"—the misuse of modern leisure is bad, even if it is nothing new. The problem to be solved, before a democratic civilization becomes possible, is how the misuse of the new kind of leisure can be avoided; and by misuse of leisure is meant any occupation of spare time which leads to a degradation of personality or of the tone of social intercourse or to a decrease in health, intelligence, or vitality of any one, owing to what he or she does in that spare time.

There are two distinct, and perhaps opposed, principles of action which we may take for our guidance in the choice of leisure occupations. On the one hand, it may be said that we have already some experience of civilized life and we ought to model ourselves upon the methods adopted in former ages. This would imply accepting the "model" on which former ages worked—the sort of "ideal life" which they worked for, when any one was free to work for it. The finest product in personality was thought, in the recent past, to be what was called a "gentleman" or a "lady." They were persons who used their leisure well; and the result of their use of leisure was the best that could be done in the architecture of character.[1] Some believe that if leisure is now extended to greater numbers, its best use would be to increase the number of gentlemen and ladies. The old model is held to be the best. The general lines of desirable human character are believed to be already laid down; and the best forms of intercourse in a civilized community are supposed to have been already discovered. Such a conception of the ideal life or character supports the belief that education in the state schools, for example, should extend to those who will have to work with their hands the sort of training which has been developed in the older traditional schools. Leisure, it is maintained, produced at best the gentleman and the lady; and extended leisure ought,

---

[1] I omit the discussion of the bourgeois ideal, largely because it seems to imply not the use but the avoidance of leisure. See Max Weber's "The Protestant Ethic" and Troelsch's "The Social Teaching of the Christian Churches."

it is said, to produce more of the same kind, although most of those who believe this also believe that a great number of gentlemen and ladies could not be produced.

On the other hand, it may be held that the principle on which our use of leisure should rest should not involve attempting to turn everybody into a lady or a gentleman on the old model. We should invent a new model—that is to say, we should be concerned not with living up to the old ideal but with establishing in practice a new ideal. That is what is meant by the phrase that "new leisure makes new men"; the new kind of leisure can make men and women just as good as the ladies and gentlemen of an earlier age, if we know what we want and have skill enough to get it. The use of leisure being the architecture of character, our new architecture ought not to be based upon the old "orders"—classical or gothic, Greek or medieval.

Those who have this attitude toward the new leisure support their argument that we must discard the gentleman and the lady as models, by pointing out that the gentleman and the lady were inventions of the recent past, like antimacassars or lace curtains. Our conceptions of a lady and a gentleman, as ideals of character and manners, were developed in the seventeenth and eighteenth centuries; although such conceptions preserved some of the characteristics of still earlier ideals—medieval ideals of knights and dames, for example. In that earlier time, however, another sort of ideal was also operative—to produce what the middle ages called "saints"—an ideal similar to the ideals of India today, in some ways very crude, in others very exalted; but the conditions under which these ideals were operative have disappeared in the modern world; and therefore new ideals must take their place. Every kind of civilization has a different conception of ideal men and women; and every such conception seems defective or even ridiculous to later ages. It would be quite possible to give one description of a medieval saint, which would be attractive, and another description which would make the saint seem foolish; and so it is with the lady and gentleman. But attractive or ridiculous, these ideals belong inevitably to the past. We are not concerned here with the actual men and women, who call themselves gentlemen and ladies, but with the *ideal* or "model" which they are trying to embody. Some of the characteristics in that ideal are charming and some ridiculous; but in any case these ideals belong to another age. Our own age, too, the modernist says, is producing its ideals. We are not all tied by our grandmothers' apron-strings.

No modernist would try to "teach his grandmother to suck eggs," but there are other subjects on which grandmothers have no right to an opinion.

The modernist has no desire to be, nor to meet an eighteenth or nineteenth century "gentleman" or "lady"; just as he has no intention whatever of being a medieval saint. Not only what we do but what we want to do is different. Not that the old model is despised; but, just as we prefer the new model of motor-car, so we may prefer a new model of man or woman. If one may speak metaphorically of a saint or a gentleman, we do not like the shape of the hood in the old model; and the old engine has a way of breaking down on a hill. We have difficulties to face or tasks to perform which cannot be performed, if the best men and women we can produce are based upon the old model. The modernist admits that, if we are not producing what the past admired, we may be doing worse; but traditionalists assume that we must be doing worse, as traditionalists in architecture, assume that, if our sculpture and architecture are not on Greek lines, they must be worse. In the fine arts, however, there are no final achievements. Modern art may yet prove to be as good as any earlier art; and the architecture or character and manners also may be as good in a new material on new lines as it ever was. What are the new lines?

They should be described, not in terms of Utopia or of some vague hope, but in terms of actual contemporary customs and attitudes. That is to say, the modern model, which replaces the old, is to be found in certain hints or indications, in shops and streets, in buses and public libraries. The modernist looks for such hints in actual life—in the actual uses of the new kind of leisure, which may indicate what men and women of to-day desire to be. This implies that the modern world is the first stage in a new kind of civilization and not merely the end of an old civilization—that we are in the spring, not in the autumn. We are looking for the new shoots, not for the dead leaves.

These, then, are the characteristics of the new model. First, he or she would be more "lively" and "energetic." A man or woman is overworking who has not as much energy and thought to use in leisure as is used at work. But if work is not in any sense enjoyable, it is exhausting; and if it is enjoyable, it is not so clearly divided from leisure, because work time and playtime pass into one another without the change being noticed. We shall never have enough energy for leisure until certain reforms take place in "work"—with which we are not concerned in this book. But even now work is less exhausting than it used to be; and the result is that every one is more "lively" in leisure. That, says the modernist, ought to be carried further.

Another characteristic of the new model is the decrease of dullness or boredom; or perhaps one ought to say the decrease of empty-mindedness. Leisure, as earlier chapters have indicated, is much fuller of opportunities for enjoyment than it used to be. There is more to be done and therefore less likelihood of being dull. Clearly there are some disadvantages incidental to this—for example, the danger of confusion and exhaustion; but it is by no means inevitable that any one should be exhausted by enjoying himself, unless he has not sense enough to stop. There is a danger in good wine; but that is nothing against good wine, nor anything in favor of no wine. Granted a little sense, the new opportunities for using leisure give variety and life to one's interests. The desire for a variety of interests drove many into towns, to escape from the monotony of the old country life; and the radio, giving new interests to those who live in country parts, has assisted to stop the flow of population into towns. Modern life is more exciting and interesting for great numbers everywhere. The modern model, therefore, is a man or woman who expects to be amused and interested. There is no reason why a good man should be a bore; but most of the professionally virtuous are bores because they are bored. Those who are amused and interested are both amusing to others and interesting to meet. The new model man or woman is light-hearted. We simply do not believe in solemnity, say the modernists.

Another aspect of the new model is enjoyment in fellowship with people one does not know. A very obvious characteristic of modern leisure is the gathering of crowds at football matches or to see any public "event." Some critics of modern life see nothing good in that; and indeed the horror of crowds has given rise to a most misleading conception of the so-called crowd mind or herd mind. Crowds are said to roar like wild beasts and to trample on things in general; but in spite of psychologists, there are good qualities in a crowd. In any case, thousands of men and women enjoy being in a crowd and feel better for it; and thousands have had experience of a cheerful crowd of people "out" to enjoy themselves. Traditionally, crowds, called "mobs," have been supposed to be destructive; and clearly such destructive crowds exist today. But the modern crowd using leisure has an entirely different character. A modern crowd at leisure keeps spontaneous order, and it may easily "bring out" what is best in a man, rather than what is worst. Community singing indicates what is possible. The delight in being with great numbers of happy people is not to be despised; and the modern man or woman will find new uses for that delight. It is not to be denied that disorder may at any moment lead to panic; but usually the immense crowds at our modern entertainments consist of individuals or groups who "arrange" themselves without confusion. Modern transport and modern advertisement has made these great crowds possible; but they would never be enjoyable to any one, if each member of the crowd did not play a part of his own in the general half-conscious plan. Indeed even psychologists would learn more about the so-called "group mind" by analysis of their own experience, rather than long-range observation of others; and it would probably be found that by such experience the modern man is learning to be at ease with all sorts of strangers. He is much less frightened of strangers than his grandfather used to be, and is therefore more companionable. Eating in common at public restaurants, as it was suggested in an earlier chapter, is playing its part in the enjoyable intercourse with strangers; but the large gatherings for games or sports carry the same tendency further.

Such experience is obviously less valuable than intimate friendship; but there is a place also for a more superficial, and yet friendly, contact with anybody and everybody. The modern man, so the modernist argues, will have that easy manner with any one he meets, which is perhaps an expression of a new confidence in other men. This stands in contrast with the aloofness of the old ideal or with the attitude toward men which was expressed in the "Imitation of Christ"—"As often as I go among men I return less a man." That is simply not true in modern experience. And again, in the old days, every true gentleman or lady would wait to be "introduced," as in Gilbert's verses about two gentlemen who were cast away on a desert island and who could not speak because they had not been introduced.[2] The new model man or woman is not so "particular."

Those who are influenced by the new ideal will be eager to share enjoyment. Public parks and public bathing pools are the products, not of gentility, but of democracy. The abolition of public executions occurred, and kindness to animals arose, not in earlier stages of civilization, but in our own. The older model of a fine fellow did, indeed, at-

---

[2] In "Etiquette":
"These passengers, by reason of clinging to a mast,
Upon a desert island were eventually cast.
They hunted for their meals as Alexander Selkirk used;
But they couldn't chat together. They had not been introduced."

tempt to avoid disagreeable smells and sounds and sights; but he only ran away into a drawing-room and left them untouched outside. It is one thing to be so sensitive that you cannot bear to see what other people suffer; it is a more modern form of sensitiveness that prevents their suffering. We could not endure to see in our streets the lepers and cripples of the Middle Ages. Indeed the mere growth of disgust at the incidental effects of drunkenness may have been one of the causes for the decrease in the amount of drunkenness. Again, our "sports" are increasingly less cruel. Such sports as are felt to be in any way cruel are obviously traditional, not modern—aristocratic, and not democratic.

But if the modern man is more sensitive and humane in his enjoyment or entertainment, he is more alive, not less alive than his forefathers. Singing requires more vitality than shouting, unless one thinks of vitality as having only one outlet at a time; for singing requires intelligent attention, as well as physical force, and intelligent attention would overstrain those who can only shout. The sensitiveness of the modern man and woman is therefore a sign that they are alive at many different points. They see and hear and smell what would simply not be noticed by their ancestors. Indeed the chief argument against the old conception of gentleman and lady is that it implied a defect in vitality. Consider, for example, the ideal of "the perfect lady." She was only half alive.[3] A little cooking and sweeping would soon have cured her of her freak religion and her appetite for psychoanalysis. There are some doubts, in the modern mind, whether even the perfect gentleman was quite alive; because he was very like an automaton for carrying clothes about. So far the modernist.

The traditionalist may reply to all this argument in favor of a new model, that the gentleman and lady have enough affability and perceptiveness; and that that is all the modernist is proposing to spread further in the community. The traditionalist says that the "real" gentleman and the "real" lady do not adopt superior airs and that there was more equality of intercourse in the old days between the squire and the farmer than there is now between the banker and the postman. He would point out that in leisure all men shared the sports of the day. But most forcibly the traditionalist would argue that there are qualities of intelligence and grace in the old ideal, which in any age are essential to the

---

[3] See the admirable study "The Lady" by Mrs. E. J. Putnam (1910). The lady is defined as "the female of the favored social class." Mrs. Putnam argues that "in contemporary society she is an archaism." "In the war between man and woman, she is a hostage in the enemy's camp."

best type of personality. There is honor, and holding your place in the line, which have been among the marks of what was called an English gentleman; and such things do not become less valuable as time goes on. "I hope you don't forget, Mr. Modernist," says the traditionalist—"that Dante and his friends discussed true gentility, long before the nineteenth century—which you seem to dislike so much." [4] The old model was not perfect—the traditionalist would argue—but we can work along that line. It is not only politeness, but the inner spirit of a serene and gracious life, which the old model indicates as desirable. And that is essential for all.

The modernist, however, replies that one at least of the peculiarities of the perfect gentleman and still more of the perfect lady was that either they did not work for a living or pretended, in leisure, that they did not. Indeed some of those who could not pretend to have nothing to do were ashamed of what they had to do; and the existence of this type indicates the weakness of the old ideal. In the new civilization, the modernist argues, men and women will "bring over," as it were, from their work the outlook they express in their leisure. They

---

[4] The reference is to Guido Cavalcanti's "Al cor gentil ripara sempre amore . . ." and Dante's "Vita Nuova." "Love and the gentle heart are one same thing." The development of the "gentleman" is however clearer in Castiglione's "Book of the Courtier."

will remain, in their leisure, coal-miners or grocers or doctors or bankers, not ashamed of the way in which they obtain their power to use leisure; and, as the modernist believes, in their leisure the arts will be given the red blood of good work, which the painting and the poetry supplied to an aristocratic society so obviously lacked. It is not, therefore, out of kindness to coal-miners that the modernist desires a civilization arising from the leisure of coal-miners; it is because only so can the arts acquire again the blood and bone of real life. Painfully "thin" and weak the drawing-room ornaments of nineteenth century art appear to the modern mind. The new men and women, who may be formed by the new leisure, have something more disturbing to do. Poems and music and pictures in the new world are not "comforting," not cures of insomnia, but realities which shake those to whom they appeal most uncomfortably awake. Such art cannot come out of the leisure of an aristocratic society.

Again, the modernist would approve the tendencies toward social equality, but neither as a leveling down nor as a leveling up, if leveling up is conceived to be the formation of a community entirely consisting of ladies and gentlemen. Indeed such a community could hardly live for an hour, because it would disregard the source of all social life in labor. The "level," if such a metaphor is allowable in the explanation of equality, is no "level" at present in existence.

Social equality, as it begins to appear in the modern world, has two aspects, one is *similarity of externals* in dress and of occupations in leisure; the other is *variety of choice* for increasing numbers. Although greater numbers tend to do the same thing, greater numbers have a larger range of choice than their forefathers had, especially in the use of leisure. From the point of view of ten out of every hundred to-day, mechanism seems to reduce the variety of choice—because, for example, the same film is to be seen in many places or the same kind of dress is more generally worn. But ninety out of every hundred to-day have no power to choose among the rarer varieties shown in Bond Street in London or in Fifth Avenue in New York. Most men, women, and children have always been compelled to "standardize" their consumption; and until very recent times to "standardize" in bare necessities—in bread and wool, not in tea and artificial silk.

What appears to "the few" as an increasing standardization in modern life is for "the many" an increasing variety of choice; but most economists and literary critics of the modern world belong to "the few." They do not see the modern world with the eyes of Mrs. Smith, the engine-driver's wife. From her point of view modern mechanism has increased the variety of choice in food, clothing, housing and the occupations of leisure. The advance toward equality, therefore, which superficially seems to imply a greater homogeneity, is actually for the majority an increase in variety in ways of living. But this increase is not, as it was in the past, achieved at the price of the segregation of a few, who alone had a large freedom of choice, from the many who were thrust down to the level of bare needs. The new civilization may decrease the range of choice in very expensive clothes; but it increases the range of choice in clothes for those with small incomes. It may decrease the number in the stalls; but it increases the number in other parts of the theater. Social equality, therefore, implies a society with a greater variety of ways of life for the vast majority than is now possible for them.

A society divided in its uses of leisure by the fact that a very few have a large range of choice and the majority have no choice, is inevitably restricted in the range of its social intercourse. Those who have no choice in their uses of leisure cannot develop skill in the variety of intercourse, which is required in meeting different persons or facing different situations. But if all are more equal in having a certain range of choice—for example, in the uses of leisure, the intercourse between all becomes more subtle and various. The general advantage which follows, is a greater store of shared experience, from which all can draw. As Tocqueville said —"If men are to remain civilized or to become so, the art of associating together must grow and improve in proportion as equality of conditions is realized." And it is here argued that equality of conditions especially in the use of leisure, is actually producing an improvement in the art of associating together.

In any civilization, however, there is a general tendency to regard certain types of life as desirable. What men and women want to do in different ages, differs very much. And if we are at the beginning of a new kind of civilization, the men and women of the new age will want to do, with their spare time, all kinds of new things. It is not merely that they will have more leisure and more possible choices in the use of it; but—if their education is successful—they will want to use leisure in new ways—in new forms of public service, new forms of social intercourse, new forms of enjoyment.

The problem of leisure is not, as some seem to believe, a problem of desperately searching for something to do. Leisure is not even understood until there is no problem as to what to do with it, because you have so much in your mind that you want to do, that all you demand is time and opportunity to do it. Many now suffer from undesired and perhaps undesirable leisure. Unemployment is bad if it means that a man has no place to fill in the life of his community—like a prisoner of war wasting his years in a camp where he cannot help his fellows. But even such undesirable leisure may be an opportunity for finding out what you want to do; and the use of it may be such as to leave a man or woman better or finer or freer in mind. One man may find greater freedom in being entertained and another in doing something for himself. But it is difficult to say that any man ought to do this or that in leisure. It is clear only that he ought to want to do something; and to want to do something is the result of education. If education, in school or after, leaves men and women with no interest at all—with nothing they want to do, apart from what they must do, then it has failed to fit them for life.

What any generation wants to do in its leisure is the expression of its characteristic ideal; and it has been shown above that there are modern views of what constitutes the best sort of man or woman.

Sketches or first "casts" of the new type are already observable; but the most valuable sketches are not the most exotic or striking. In a world of "publicity," what is valuable can more easily lie hidden—happily for the success of a new venture. Journalism and the art of advertising are protections for what is really valuable precisely because they concentrate attention upon what is superficial, just as the fast motor-car which keeps to the main road, is a protection for the quiet of forest paths; and it is an added amusement for those who know "the real thing" to see the pursuit of the sham modern which revives, in those who are both "smart" and "young," the most primitive types of the caveman. But outside the range of reporters and beyond the shining of film stars, the new models of men and women are being built into the foundations of a new community.

XIII

CAN DEMOCRACY BE CIVILIZED?

THE types of man and woman most admired and the community which is regarded as desirable may be very different from any former ideals; but the question remains whether this new democratic community could produce a civilization as fine as any in the past. It is assumed that democracy means not merely a political or economic system, but a social or cultural relationship, which is based upon the assumption that every one shall be treated as equal in order to discover who is best at each job. Nobody now believes that men are equal in ability; but some of us believe that in ninety-nine out of every hundred parts of them, all men are very similar and that the value of the one hundredth part in which each differs cannot be discovered unless every one has a more equal opportunity than is now possible. In modern leisure, as it was argued above, there is a tendency toward this equalization of opportunities. Many more than hitherto have at least a chance of discovering whether, for example, music can affect them deeply. In earlier times those with small incomes had more equal chances in the enjoyment of games than in the enjoyment of music. A man may be deaf to music; and he may derive from "sport" all that he can obtain from any enjoyment. In his case nothing is gained, if opportunities for the enjoyment of music are given to him. But we cannot assume that such opportunities will be valueless for any other person. There are varieties of ability, which show themselves in reaction to different opportunities; and modern leisure gives a greater variety of opportunities for "bringing out" what may be in a man. In that sense it is democratic. But is it "civilized"?

Civilization may depend for its roots upon the way in which work is done; but it depends for its finest flower upon the use of leisure. When we ask, therefore, whether a democracy can be civilized, we do not mean to ask only whether we can abolish slums, nor only whether there can be more telephones per head of the population or more motor-cars and fewer horses—although all these things are important as roots of a particular form of civilized life. The question is whether modern leisure—as it has been described—can produce personalities as fine or works of art as great as those, for example, of ancient Athens or ancient China—without the invariable accompaniment of such ancient civilizations, a class of men and women who were merely the instruments of "the good life" of a few. But even to ask such a question implies a conception of the place of leisure in the whole of a man's life with which all may not agree. Let us grant that it is impossible to find out what the "place" of leisure in life ought to be unless the rest of life is what it ought to be. Exhausting or ill-paid or insecure work contaminates and spoils the leisure with which it is accompanied. Those who are "unemployed"—in our modern sense of that word—are depressed and constrained—tied sometimes by regulations which degrade the quality of what might seem to be their leisure. But the majority are not "unemployed" in that sense. The place of leisure in the life of those who work for a living is the problem of the modern world, which is fundamental in discussing the future of civilization. Leisure for such people is, first, a relief—a standing aside and an escape. It is not only a rest for recovering energy in order to do more work; it has its own value as a time for free growth or development, in entertainment or in enjoying oneself. But now the argument must go further than that. What a man does in his leisure changes the tone or atmosphere of the whole of the society in which he lives; and it may change the whole current of human experience. Think, for example, of the leisure of the Athenians, when the roots of common life blossomed into great drama. Such examples may seem to be too bookish, too "traditional"; and indeed perhaps if all the Greek plays were lost, we should more easily discover what the theater is. Certainly if Greek music had not been lost, our music to-day would be as bad as our architecture is. The Greek type of leisure and its best uses may actually prevent our seeing what can be derived from modern leisure. In any case, whether they are Athenian or not—works of fine art are the flowers of civilized leisure; that is to say, actual poems and symphonies. And if democracy is to be civilized, works of fine art as well as a deeper scientific insight must come out of the leisure of those who work for a living. Why?

The reason can most easily be explained by a parable of common life. Every one lives in the ordinary world of breakfast and dinner most of his time. It is a good world, if the dinner is good; and it is foolish to despise it as trivial. But it is not the only world. Every one of those with whom the argument is concerned lives also in a more spacious "other" world—which is the world in which one works for a living. That is the world of the streets of the city of common life. But such a city has walls; and in the walls are gates through which men go for holiday. Close under the walls outside are the playing fields; and in their leisure most men stop there. One should hesitate to urge any one who is satisfied with the playing fields to go farther from the city of common life; for such a man might not have the sort of ears and eyes required in the more dangerous forest land beyond the playing fields. But some in their leisure go beyond, into the unexplored "other" world; and a very few of these bring back what are called works of art, as men bring back from their sleep the faded memory of a dream. Let us leave these out of account. They have genius. They are poets or other artists. But you and I, who are not poets, nor painters, nor composers of great music—we too can go, in our leisure, and some of us actually do go, into that frontier world—beyond the city and beyond the playing fields. One goes out by the path called music; and another by the path called poetry. The "place" of leisure in the life of any one who goes so far is somehow different from the place of leisure in the life of a man who does not leave the city or, at any rate, does not go far beyond the walls. But do not suppose that those who have "frontier" habits are superior beings; for some of them are railwaymen and textile workers. Such men and women cannot help doing what they do. They do not listen to music because somebody told them that they ought to do it. They do not read poetry in order to shine in conversation. They do not even think, except when they can't help it. Some say we ought to make everybody think—even those who don't want to think; but I don't agree. Thinking is most unsatisfactory! If you can't help thinking, then you have an excuse; but if you don't want to think—you may burst if you try. If there is nothing in music for you, then leave music and all that sort of thing alone! However, if you want to listen to what other people enjoy—perhaps that will not do you much harm; although what you hear then is not music at all. Many have been to concerts who have never heard music. It is implied in this view of the arts and the frontier holiday from which they come that the "real" world is not altogether a world of breakfast and dinner. Other parts of it that are real enough, but not quite obvious, are revealed in the explorations of science and the forms of art. And leisure is the part of most men's lives in which some hear and see and feel what is not obvious. No sane man lives on the frontier. A sane man comes back to the world of breakfast and dinner; but he comes back somehow different. The spirit of a man needs holiday as well as his body. As Flecker puts it:

CAN DEMOCRACY BE CIVILIZED? 245

Four great gates has the city of Damascus
And four grand wardens, on their spears reclining,
All day long stand, like tall stone men,
And sleep on the towers when the moon is shining.

This is the Song of the South Gate Holder,
A silver man, but his song is older.
O spiritual pilgrim rise: the night has grown her single horn,
The voices of the souls unborn are half adream with Paradise.

God be thy guard from camp to camp: God be thy guide from well to well:
God grant beneath the desert stars Thou hear the prophet's camel bell.

But now I must break in unkindly and prevent your going any further on that pilgrimage at the moment. I can imagine somebody saying— "That's all very well, but what has that to do with the modern world? The modern world is an abominable collection of vulgar film-stories, of motor-cars that kill people on the roads, of noise and hurry. Democracy is merely a sentimental veil thrown over vulgarity." Let us see how much truth there is in this view of the modern world. It is a much more subtle attack upon modern habits than the mere objection to going about faster or seeing more. It implies that what used to be called the inner life of a man is being exhausted by modern conditions—that we are being "externalized"—that there is no place in a modern world for the leisure which produces the finest personalities and the greatest works of art. It is argued that even leisure is so much occupied with "doing" things that people have no time nor inclination for the quiet beyond the reach of the cries of the city and its playing fields. Even in our schools we have overdone the occupations of leisure. I can imagine the loud laughter with which some old philosopher would greet the statement that in modern education children are taught to play! It is bad enough to fill the hours out of school with what is called homework; but worse still, the new generation is being made restless by never being left to itself, even for its play. And again, among the traditional leisured class, leisure was filled with strenuous and exhausting exercise, because they had no other outlet for energy. But now thousands of those who work hard enough, "play" still harder and exhaust themselves on holiday, because they cannot think of doing nothing. Short of actual exhaustion some people think that they are using leisure "profitably" by seeing more "sights" and enduring endless discomfort in travel. It is all very well to get as much out of life and the world as one can; but the illusion which is preventing the growth of civilized life in the modern world is this "externalism"—this restless passion for being entertained.

What is the reply? I do not think we can deny the truth of the charge against the dominant tendency of to-day in the use of leisure. But something else is growing under the surface of movie-going and motor tours; and that something else is just as significant of the modern world as the superficial noise and hurry. First, the inner life, as it is called, need not be exhausted by going in a motor-bus, any more than it was by going in a farm-cart. There are some whose inner life cannot survive modern conditions; but such people altogether overestimate the influence of modern conditions on other people. A man may be as calm, as far aloof from "externalism" in the midst of the modern current of life as other men were in the simpler circumstances of earlier times. The security of what used to be called an "inner" life is not to be found in the refusal to live in the modern world, but in the plunge right down into the midst of it all. This reply means that the charge of "externalism" is turned against the critics of the modern world themselves. They themselves, so the reply runs, have made the mistake of identifying the modern world with what is merely its external form. They see the motor-bus and the movie and not the inner force of thought and imagination which made such things available. In earlier times they would have condemned forks, because fingers were better for picking up food and men might lose their heads in the desire to possess forks. Some in our own day lose their heads about motor-cars and moving pictures; but the best way of curing that is to improve their heads, not to destroy the films. Similarly, what is called "democracy" may be mere absorption in mechanisms, mere externalism, universal vulgarity; but it may not be that.

The critic of the modern world then says: "Well, if democracy may not be vulgarity, is there any sign that it will not be? Even if democracy may be civilized, is there any reason in actual experience to hope that it will be?" The reply is to be found in the tone of mind or the mental attitude of some at least of those who use modern circumstances—who actually go to the movies and sit in motor-buses. Those who reply to the critic would say that personalities as fine come out of the movies as out of some other older places which need not be named. Men and women and children are not made into gangsters or sexual maniacs by film stories, and if one were to ask most of them about the effect of the films upon their characters they would probably not find much to say in reply. Indeed a certain number of those who are familiar with the modern world are far less deeply affected by its superficial aspects than critics suppose. Even the sense of change which used in earlier times to make men sigh over a world which seemed worthless because it was transitory, has another meaning now. To the modern mind, the world is worth attention precisely because it is transitory; for only so can it be amenable to our control of it. We stand above the change.

There is no reason whatever for being carried away. The aëroplane which may carry my body fast and far may leave my mind unmoved. The rush of the traffic or the whirl of machinery may not enter into the deeper recesses of a person who is civilized. Indeed civilization, at its very best, is this capacity for being in a world and not "of" it. And that is in our hands. No man is swept away by the stream of events, unless in ignorance of his own power to stand aside; and some men and women and children in the midst of the modern world do actually remain calm at the core of their spirits.

The finest use of leisure is this standing aside. In such use of leisure we attain the "quiet" or serenity in which the most intimate converse with other persons and the clearest perception of the world around us is achieved. There is, indeed, in all men some capacity for standing aside. We are not only players on the stage, but also parts of the audience. We can watch ourselves playing our parts. And some few men and women have this capacity for standing aside in an exceptional degree. They are not therefore aloof, nor "superior"; but they are less easily moved, although not less deeply moved than other folk who laugh and cry more readily. This type has always existed and it still exists in the midst of the modern world. The problem of our civilization, especially in its uses of leisure, is whether the influence or vitality of this type is swamped or destroyed by the increase of entertainments and the rush and hurry of a world which has an appetite for change. Can we "afford" machinery and all it implies? Can civilized life survive an over-supply of the possible means of civilization? As against the critic of modern life, it is maintained that, in fact, civilized life does survive and grow in the modern world—that the quality of the intercourse which is the life of a community has actually improved since common folk have had more leisure and more uses of leisure. Consider the kindliness of common folk in the streets. Look at those who go out of the towns on holiday for quiet. If they are few, they are none the less a sign of a new civilization; and it is the civilization of equals at ease in converse with all sorts of men and women.

That a great civilization is now being born is shown by the new quality of that inner life which is possible in it. The methods by which an inner life arises and flourishes are not necessarily those of the past; and indeed some of the methods of the past are futile. The hermits of Egypt in early Christianity were wrong; but historical discussion of such attempts may obscure the main issue. At any rate the hermit's way is not the only way. The preservation of serenity by an élite, which is freed from the necessities of daily labor or the religion of a "clerus" aloof from domestic or other personal relationships —these also are not the only ways, nor necessarily better than ours. But methods are not our subject here. The important fact in the modern world is the existence of an inner life, which common folk share. As a modern novelist puts it:

> Every man who is not a devil, has his own retreat, his intact island, ringed about with the waters of the spirit, where he may live his own life and not be pursued: and from which he may set out on his voyages. A saint vanishes thither continually; he walks upon the waters: the hounds check and lose him: while they are sniffing the earth, he is gone. The simple have an island in their simplicity; children, whom our blind knowledge seeks to encompass, in the starry jungle of their imagination: and some find

refuge in the natural miracles, in their secret woods and mountains, to which they flee, not to praise beauty that is of the eye, but to reaffirm a fealty of the soul, obeying joyfully in the midst of life that material summons of dust to dust which, like death's compassionate trumpet, is a supreme release from all claims. . . . In every great work of art an artist dies and rises again; and we, who enter into its illusion, die to this world and are reborn. . . . [And again] . . . Life does not consist in outward acts and is little affected by them. It is an inward and secret experience which those who become aware of it—and they are few except in childhood and perhaps in great age—seek to intensify, for to intensify is to protect and sustain it.[1]

Is that "modern"? Contemporary literary criticism seems to imply that "modern" literature is only the psychoanalysis of sexual mania or the incoherence of a mythological "subconscious." But to use the word "modern" in that sense is precisely the "externalism" which is supposed by old-fashioned writers to be a defect of modernity. In a more generous sense of the word, the expression of the contemporary sense of the inner life is modern; for the characteristics of the modern world lie at the heart of it: and there is in the use of aëroplanes and movies, an inner life actually enjoyed.

Here then we come back to the argument in the earlier part of this chapter, where it was suggested

[1] Charles Morgan's "The Fountain," pp. 227, 309.

that leisure is an opportunity for hearing and seeing and feeling realities that are not obvious in the world of breakfast and dinner. Such realities were seen in earlier civilization, and the record of what was seen is in their science and philosophy and their works of art—their poems, their melodies. These are still valuable, in so far as we can look through them at our world—not only our world of breakfast and dinner, but also our "other" worlds. In our world too, is the frontier—the horizon of experience; there are the realities we call death and life, and that other reality, which is sometimes called personal love—material for poetry, which science can hardly touch. All such things are not in regions far away, unreachable by common folk; but sometimes very close. In leisure one may find them almost at one's door. Education, in school and after, ought to be able to give to all at least the ability to face such things once in a while. But that implies a place for leisure as the source of one's philosophy of life—if one may call by that long name the common sense of ordinary people. Such people have a sense of things which they never put into words; but why should they? What is in words?

You are now reading certain words in print and the print would equally well be seen by a dog. But for you, and not for the dog, there is something "in" the words which is called "meaning." It is not the print. You cannot see it, nor bottle it up, if the language we now speak is lost. It is part of "me"; and the meaning of what I write is as "real" as the print. But there is more or less of meaning for you in what is printed here, in proportion as your experience and mine are the same or different. This "meaning" is not any more mine than it is yours, when you understand it. One step more . . . I have been trying to say certain things about leisure and the modern world, and not half of what I meant came out of the words I used. The words pointed to parts of your experience; but they remained inadequate to "carry over" the inmost reality in the experience of each of us. So it is with all the forms of art, not only speech. The effort to express a new meaning is often crude; but the source of that art—the life underlying the expression—is the common life of the modern world.

Look back then at the course of the argument; and find more meaning in it. Outside of working hours the daily habits of most men and women have been changed during the past thirty years. Not only in politics and economics, but also in the study of social custom, new fashions in food and dress and houses are important, because they affect men's characters. The greatest changes, however, have been the result of new methods of entertainment and new ways of enjoying oneself; and the movie, the motor, betting, and hiking must all be allowed for in the making of our characters. But the changes which have occurred by accident have been accompanied by certain movements which have changed the attitude of men and women. These movements are restricted to this or that particular reform, and they all seem to point to a new ideal—a new kind of conception as to what is best. The dominant new tendency is toward equality, but that goes with a much more widespread feeling for other people and, as I have tried to show—it implies also a desire for the sort of enjoyment which is quiet and rarely found. We are moving, as I conclude, toward a much freer and subtler community between all men. The forms of that common life have a place for the arts and for scientific insight. The meaning, which is carried to strange places by these words, is more generally heard, and therefore more alive in the whole of human intercourse. But not all that I mean gets into the words or gets over to you. Something more is put into the common store of thought or emotion by you who read—in so far as in these words you understand—not me but the worlds—the many worlds you live in. And round the whole of what has been written and what you have understood are the hints and implications—the atmosphere or tone which is the frontier of words.

No one discovers what leisure can be entirely from somebody else's discussion of it. In all this region of life, the frontier of experience cannot ever be completely explored; and even what is seen there by any one can never be adequately expressed. Leisure is the time for going beyond what men know of life or can say of it; and so—if it will not seem to be too obscure a conclusion—I come to the end of what I have to say, because only a poet could say more and even he could not say everything. I shall quote an old philosopher, Sextus Empiricus, for my conclusion: "That man is wise who even by his silence pays honor to what is divine in the world, if he knows why he is silent."

XIV

PUBLIC POLICY

THE description of changes in the use of leisure during the past half-century, and the discussion of the issues involved leave the way open for the formulation of public policy. It was remarked at the beginning of this book that leisure had been treated hitherto as a worthless by-product; but even so, new social tendencies have arisen out of the recent increase in the uses of leisure. The kind of public policy, which might be adopted in view of these tendencies, will naturally depend upon whether they are approved or condemned. Some hate the results of movie and radio, of cheap clothing, and more varied food for those with small incomes; and such opponents of recent tendencies will find much more to condemn in the modern world than has been condemned in this book. Also these objectors and opponents are the more influential, the wealthier, the privileged—those who have been educated in the more expensive schools and universities. The situation could be expressed in still clearer terms; but there is no special advantage in calling a spade a spade, if one's meaning is sufficiently clear to those whom one is addressing. The accumulation of past prestige and power stands against any policy which seeks to extend the advantages of the new situation to all members of any community.

On the other hand, those who would, in the main, approve of contemporary tendencies in the use of leisure, see in those tendencies the destruction of traditionalism, localism, and caste or class distinctions. They are objectors not against tradition but against a traditionalism, which is the unreasonable worship of tradition; they are opponents not of local patriotism but of segregate barbarism. They dislike inherited class divisions, but not the social recognition of differences of personal quality. From the new opportunities of a much increased leisure for those who work for a living, they hope to develop a freer companionship between all members of any community, open-mindedness with respect to new ideas and new customs and a much greater quickness of reaction to any circumstances which may arise. Public policy in the minds of those who approve of modern tendencies would naturally reinforce them.

In early times and in simpler societies than ours,

public policy with respect to leisure is dominated by ecclesiastical or other religious organizations. The earliest Rest Days appear to have been days on which it was unlucky or dangerous to carry on one's usual occupation.[1] They were taboo: and the Hawaiians are said to have called the missionaries' Sunday "le tabu." But the confusion of solemnity with riotous rejoicing seems to have begun long ago. Rest days became feast days. The ostensible reasons given for both worship and rejoicing were religious; for the priest chose the days and controlled their uses. Such control survives in some circles in European and American society; but it has had very little effect upon the social changes of the past fifty years. The many churches and other religious bodies disagree among themselves as to the proper seasons of leisure and the proper uses of leisure; and therefore ecclesiastical influences to-day cancel themselves out. No one desiring to modify or control public policy in the use of leisure to-day would look to the churches as his instruments of policy. These instruments must clearly be the state, industrial organizations, and educational institutions.

The present number of public holidays and the

---

[1] For details, see Hutton Webster's "Rest Days," Macmillan, N. Y., 1916.

common use of them, however, is still due to the ecclesiastical tradition which in the Western world is an amalgamation of Greek and Roman custom with Hebraic regulations. In ancient Egypt, it seems, holidays amounted to one fifth of the year; in ancient Athens there were fifty to sixty days of festival in the year; and at Tarentum in the days of its prosperity there were more holidays than working days. In ancient Rome about one third of the days of the year were *nefasti*, unlucky for work; and in the later Empire, the "games" and other festivals were largely extended. That is one part of our tradition. On the other hand, the Hebrew tradition of the Sabbath seems to have arisen out of a new-moon festival; and the contradiction between solemnity and riot goes far back even in that tradition, obscured as its history is by the meticulous regulations of rabbis. The medieval system replaced the Greek-Roman festivals by Saints' Days and toned down the crudity of the Jewish Sabbath. We have now, by a series of accidents, reduced the number of Greek-Roman festivals and preserved the regularity of the Hebraic tradition; so that we have in the Western world about sixty days of public holiday in a year—that is to say, only about half the number that was common in most highly civilized societies in the past.

The reduction in the number of Saints' Days, treated as holidays, is directly due to the "worldly asceticism" which over-estimated the importance of work. The effort to correct this asceticism was made in the early industrial period in the legislation on "bank" holidays or other public holidays, largely with a view to giving workers the rest which was supposed to improve their capacity for work. Even machinery was seen to need rest; but this was not real holiday. It was a survival of primitive conceptions of work. In primitive conditions to cease work meant to reduce the supply of bare needs; and all through human history good men have feared idleness, because all lived in continual danger of starvation or physical want. That fear lies behind the tradition of "saving." Unless we "save" a surplus from this harvest, we may starve; for the next harvest may fail. That feeling is the survival in our bones of the fear in which our ancestors lived. And even to-day when "capital" lies idle in plant and land and bank deposits, the dead hand of the past reaches up in the effort to "save." So we continue with the ancient fear lest "work" should not be done—like men who have labored so hard to avoid danger that they cannot rest when the danger is past. We are pursued by ghosts, in our economic and social policy.

But while we dream in our public policy, the whole situation has been transformed. New machinery and new power-supplies and the stores of knowledge waiting to be applied for still greater production, if it is needed—all this has destroyed the ground for our ancestral fears. There is no danger in the reduction of work. Rest days are no longer the barely necessary intervals for recuperation in order to do more work. We have power now that no former ages had; and we have reserves of power still unused. The whole basis of public policy therefore should have changed, especially with regard to leisure. We can "afford" abundant leisure for all.

A great increase in leisure and its uses, however, can take place only if the whole industrial system is generally felt to have changed its character; and at present neither industrialists nor politicians seem to have grasped that the situation is new. The new machinery and the new power-supply seem to have made no impression upon those who direct finance, industry, or the political parties—perhaps because these men are, in general, in old age and were already old before the transformation occurred. But perhaps the reason is still more subtle. It may be that the mind of to-day in public affairs is not able to grasp the new situation because it has no language which fits the facts. All our economic science assumes the ancient conditions—an increasing population pressing upon the sources of supply; and all our politics assume the local territorial sovereign as the source of order and justice. Indeed it may be that our governing assumptions, embodied in all languages, are those of a slave society, as they were for Plato and Aristotle. But the difficulty need not be explained further. Certainly there is a difficulty; for public policy based upon the facts of the modern world is not yet even understood, much less generally supported. Such public policy would, in the most general terms, involve: (1) decrease of time and energy spent in production in all countries; (2) increase of public provision for education and uses of leisure; and (3) the acceptance in practice of the principle that "the good life" is for each and for all members of all communities—for Chinese and Africans as well as for bankers in London and New York.

Public policy based upon these conceptions will aim first at a great increase in the amount of leisure among those who work in industry. The eight hour day was an ideal of the reformers in industry at the end of the World War; and among the first conventions agreed upon at the first conference of the new International Labor Organization was one which attempted to define this ideal in terms which might make it realizable. The British governments ever since that date (1919) have all found reasons why this reform should not be introduced. In some countries in Europe it was introduced for a time and partially. But on the whole British workers already have an eight-hour day; and since the War in many other countries hours of work have been reduced by other means than legislation. The fundamental issue is not legislation. It is social custom.

Already some recognition of the importance of leisure is to be found in the "welfare" and "sports" organizations of private firms. These have obviously increased in the past half-century. Secondly, the International Labor Organization at its conference in 1924 discussed "the Utilization of the Workers' Leisure" and many resounding platitudes are to be found in the official publications connected with that conference. Thirdly, the two successful dictatorships, in Russia and Italy, have paid special attention to leisure. In Russia the movies, radio, sports, and games are all organized centrally under the Communist party. Great advance has been made in the development of popular taste and in healthy activities in leisure, especially if the present situation is compared not with that of countries in the democratic tradition but with pre-war

Russia, in which drinking vodka and attending church services seem to have been the only uses of leisure supported by public organization. In Italy the pre-war situation was not so undeveloped; for many associations for sport and drama already existed before Fascism developed. But great advance has been made there too, under the "Opera Nazionale Dopolavoro." [2] This is a central Fascist organization for the assistance of local clubs for sport, travel, education, music, and drama. In non-authoritarian countries there are many more sports, games, and other occupations of leisure; but although in some cases supported out of public funds, they are not usually dependent upon public policy. There are advantages in spontaneous organization for the use of leisure, as will be shown later; but in any case public policy is required for the provision of opportunities for those with small incomes. In the first place, therefore, public policy must promote the decrease of hours of work, because that can be done only by general agreement. It does not follow that every one or even the majority should have leisure at the same time. Public policy must therefore increase the opportunities for attending movies or playing games, even if this involves work

---

[2] See Schneider and Clough's "Making Fascists," p. 182, and the Official Report of the Dopolavoro.

for attendants. The main purpose is to transfer much of the energy now used in work time to uses of leisure.

In the second place, public policy must extend the period of education throughout adolescence. It has been shown above that adolescence involves special problems in the modern world, because of the rapid social and industrial changes which may seriously affect the plastic emotions and intelligence of youth. The need for labor is no longer an excuse for permitting children to leave school at twelve or fourteen; and as life, in a healthier population, is longer, the preparation for it should be longer. Obviously this does not imply a mere continuance of what goes on now in schools, for a few more dismal years. A new method and a new organization of education would be needed. The uses of leisure would be, in a modern education, much more prominently in the minds of teachers than the different forms of work for which the new generation may have to be prepared. But here again a change in method would have to be made; because the methods used in the education of the leisured class in the old society would be quite unsuitable as a model for the new education. A different kind of leisure is in question. Such a leisure would be, for example, not much concerned with games but largely devoted to creative arts of all kinds.

Perhaps the later years of such education would not be spent in schools at all, but in fields and factories. In any case, the training would be "occupational" in basis and would aim at a general development of social capacities. The most important change in a longer period of education, however, would be the formation during adolescence of a generation of men and women able to think and act for themselves. The traditional education is largely a training in "waiting for orders" or swallowing what is provided. The education of "upper classes" has been very largely of that kind, partly indeed because it is to the advantage of those who enjoy privileges in any social system to maintain even in themselves those virtues which tend to conserve rather than to change that system. But a more radical education would prepare new generations to change what they have inherited; and the first step in that preparation is the inclination to criticize what has been already thought or done. Only those fear criticism who have a suspicion that what may be criticized is not true.

The value of leisure, from this point of view, is in that it is the opportunity for thinking and doing what is not "useful," at any rate in any immediate application. The free play of the minds of common folk has hardly yet been understood. Obviously only a few, in each generation, will add to the supreme achievements in the sciences or the arts; but quite apart from the fact that these few may be children of any sort of workers, the rest add something in the simplest arts and sciences of common life, if they have time and energy and educated perception to use in the world of breakfast and dinner. It is this free play of the intelligence and emotion of ordinary folk, upon subjects that are not "useful" or "practical," that education should produce.

Again, public policy for leisure would provide many more opportunities for enjoyment. In Great Britain and the United States public libraries, museums and galleries, public parks, and public baths are the highest achievements of recent policy. In some German and Italian towns there are also public opera-houses and theaters. But the modern world is only at a beginning in such provisions for leisure; and two traditional misconceptions prevent any adequate policy being adopted in the public provision of new facilities for using leisure. One misconception is that such public provision is a form of charity for those with low incomes. It seems to be imagined that public baths, for example, are for "the poor"; and even public libraries are avoided by those who can afford to support a private firm of book-distributors. This is ridiculous. A tennis club is not a charity for its members; what each wants can be supplied only by coöperation among many. And so public provision of parks or baths or libraries is coöperation for what cannot be had otherwise. The second misconception is that public provision of services of any sort should be for "necessities" or a "bare minimum." It may be desirable that "nobody should have cake until everybody has bread," but public policy should include provision for cake. For one thing, we must keep alive the taste for cake, while we are proceeding with a better distribution of bread. But the actual policy which is best depends upon the circumstances of time and place. The question here is one of general principle. The public provision of "luxuries" is essential in a policy of leisure; and it has been shown above that recent transformations of production make it quite possible to transfer public attention from bare necessities to future possibilities of a much higher level of general well-being. Thus a much greater provision for what is not "necessary," for the use of all, is the natural foundation of a new order consonant with our new powers.

Fundamentally, indeed, it is implied in the reasoning so far used that public policy in the modern world should envisage as its purpose a "good life" not for a few only but for all; and this "good life" for all includes, as it did in the conception of the Greek philosophers, not only food and clothing but also the enjoyment of knowledge and the arts. So long as a community is felt to be divided into those who "work" and those who have leisure—so long, that is, as the slave-society of Greek times is perpetuated in the atmosphere of education and general culture—so long will it be possible to confine public policy to the provision of the bare necessities for work. For it will be assumed, if not consciously stated, that what are not bare necessities can be obtained by those who should obtain them without public help. Thus stage-plays and the finest music can be left to be enjoyed by those who can "afford" it. Certainly it is not "necessary" that a railwayman or a postman should enjoy Beethoven; for he will run a train or deliver letters just as well without such enjoyment—and indeed Beethoven might "distract" him! The "good life" is thus left to be acquired at a price beyond the reach of the majority; and public provision supplies only as much as will make "workers" do more work. In direct opposition to this, it is suggested here that public provision should be made for the enjoyment by every member of a community of the whole of the "good life."

But this implies a practice, in legislation, industrial organization, and administration, that aims at giving the charwoman the opportunity to hear Beethoven, not in order that she may do more work but because she is a woman. It implies giving to the African and Indian education for the escape from dependence upon our noble selves. And it implies the extension of a sense of community with common folk in all lands among all those who have influence or direct policy anywhere. But this is revolutionary; and it is still conceived to be improper to suggest revolution as public policy.

XV

PRIVATE ENTERPRISE

ENTERPRISE, in the traditional use of the word, means the ability to produce or to organize production so as to derive gain from such ability. And by a series of unconscious mental changes, it is easily believed that such enterprise is necessarily "private," for ability is individual. The confused and primitive psychology embodied in the language of current economic science, however, does not concern us here. It is useful only to note that "enterprise" has never been connected with "consumption" or use. It has never seemed to economists to be praiseworthy that any one has good taste or that any one is active in changing his taste; and yet it is the use and not the production of the new transport and the new material goods which transformed the nineteenth century. To be enterprising in the adoption of new fashions or new ways of living is not yet very common. Indeed if it became too common, an industrial upheaval would occur. What would happen, for example, to the capital and plant and labor engaged in making hats, if hats ceased to be worn? The suggestion that the public taste for weapons of destruction might be changed by a policy of disarmament already throws the armament firms into a frenzy. The Doukobors, who go about naked, are too "enterprising" for the clothing trades. But clearly there is a sense in which enterprise and even private enterprise is good, in "consumption."

As the majority certainly do not suffer from too much of this enterprise, the cynic might advise them to do what they already do—to follow the fashion; and yet it may be good to increase the tendency of a few to make new experiments in the use of modern opportunities, especially in leisure. This would be "private" enterprise. Indeed it is wrong to suppose that any individual is helpless. The sense of the oppression which is due to the social system, makes reformers look too exclusively to public policy as a source of improvement in existing conditions. It is true that many wrongs cannot be remedied without public action. It is true that "charity" tends to delay such action by seeming falsely to remove the ground for it. A starving man is given a meal; and the system which caused the starvation is left untouched. There is no excuse for avoiding a public policy. But when all is said as to the need for a public policy, it remains true that the new uses of leisure must be discovered in "private enterprise," by each person for himself. Indeed the chief value of leisure in the history of civilization has been that it provided opportunity for each man to go his own way without injury to others. One's work is necessarily fixed by others, since it is the service of others. Leisure is one's own.

It is implied that enough energy and imagination exist in common folk to be employed in leisure, if opportunities are provided. That is indeed the assumption implied even in public policy; for it is futile to make playgrounds, if nobody wants to play. That assumption must be implied even in a dictatorship which decides not only what opportunities should be provided but also what games should be played. Something more, however, is implied in the democratic assumption that common men "go of themselves"; for if the source of progress is believed to be in common folk, it is implied that each man already has some energy and imagination in use, even within the limits of narrow circumstances. No doubt, the pressure of such energy upon those limits is the source of reform; but the existing energy and imagination, not obstructed by the social system, is to be considered here. In every society, some enjoy themselves; although there are others who would be discontented even in a heaven of their own design. Those who make the best of what they have, however, are not necessarily opponents of reform, just as prisoners of war, who sing in their confinement, are not necessarily opposed to an end of the war.

Singing in confinement is not to be despised. But the situation in most people's leisure to-day is not so bad as that would imply, for we are less closely confined in leisure than we are at work. The first step, therefore, in using leisure is to learn how far the area of freedom in it at present extends. Most men can do more than they now do with their leisure; and besides, they can do what is different. Indeed the cry against the domination of the crowd mind is largely a cry against part of one's self; for nobody is quite so much dominated by current customs as he thinks or feels that he is. It is an illusion that we are oppressed by modern conditions, compelling us to be like every one else; not modern conditions but survivals of tradition in us, as individuals, prevent us from doing to-day what we never did before. But even the few who are imaginative tend to play games or read books from day to day exactly as they are accustomed to do. Habit in leisure saves time, as habit saves energy at work. It is useful to rely upon the old experience that one enjoys dancing or reading novels. But not one in a thousand imagines new possibilities of enjoyment; and yet if new possibilities were tried, leisure would become fuller and more significant. The first step in the improvement of the uses of leisure is a step which any one can make for himself. Any one can try something new.

Obviously there is already a tendency in human society to try new ways of using leisure. In the recently built housing areas, for example, in Great Britain, associations are sometimes formed for games or entertainments; and in some cases community centers have been created. Such groupings stand in contrast with the local organization of government, although historically, in the English tradition at least, local government was a spontaneous organization. The spontaneity has now gone out of it. The electoral and representative system has removed the local council from the range of interest of most citizens; and if their citizenship is supposed to consist only in their voting, it is obviously futile to expect them to be active in public affairs in the intervals between elections. But the community center and the community council are created by any persons who feel so disposed. The rest remain as they were before, asleep to common purposes. These community councils usually organize opportunities for leisure—playgrounds, etc., and promote new ways of using leisure—for example, amateur drama, music, and games. They are signs of a common tendency toward the discovery of new uses of leisure.

Again, clubs are spontaneous associations presenting to some men and women ideas as to using leisure which they would never have discovered for themselves. The most civilized forms of enjoyment in leisure are those which occur in social intercourse; and clubs for games or travel or the promotion of study in common are spontaneous efforts of ordinary people to find new outlets for their energies. Such spontaneous groupings for entertainment are closely connected psychologically with "Jacobin Clubs" and other sources of revolution in public affairs; for some men and women enjoy reforming the world or trying to do so. In the democratic tradition such community councils and clubs arise spontaneously and do not require to be created or organized from a center, as in the authoritarian tradition under dictatorships.

It can hardly be denied, however, that the range of uses of modern leisure is not very large. The films and radio have added to the old possibilities; hiking and gambling have been recently increased;

but there are still thousands of men, women, and children who "can't think what to do" with their leisure. It ought not to be assumed that if any one does nothing, he is wasting his time; but that will be discussed later. First, it must be shown that the feeling of boredom is an enslavement, not due to external conditions, but to defects of civilization in a person's own "inner" life. Indeed the rich are the chief sufferers from boredom. They could "afford," in the economic sense, to do what they can't think of doing.[1] Similarly at any level of income, what can be done is generally much more than what one can think of doing. There are possibilities of enjoyment in all circumstances and capacities for enjoyment in every person, which are missed because of lack of skill. These possibilities and capacities are to be discovered by extending actual enjoyments, experimentally. For example, a man may actually enjoy some music; he will discover other music which he also enjoys by cultivating or giving free play to the enjoyment he already has. He may find that this music or that has no appeal; but he may on the other hand, find some music enjoyable, which he had not formerly heard. Again, in travel new uses of leisure are discovered by visits to new

[1] The affected pessimism or Byronism of the early nineteenth century and the "tone" in Tchchov's dramas were signs of decay in a leisured class.

places in new company; indeed the number of new ways of enjoyment which are open to any one in any circumstances is infinite.

Enough has now been said to indicate the basis in experience for the general principle that leisure is the opportunity for exploration in new fields of living. If, therefore, leisure is increasing and ought to increase still further, there should be still more exploration of new fields and still less traditionalism. The production of necessaries or of standardized goods has become more mechanical. Repetition work is increasing. It is our method of supplying a non-oligarchic market. But as work time involves more repetition processes, leisure should allow of the corrective—more tendency to vary. Differences of individuality or personality may become less important for most work in production for exchange; but such differences of personality thereby become more important for "consumption" in leisure. Therefore each person ought to make experiments in leisure, beyond what he has usually done.

Such experimenting or exploration is the salvation of civilized life. In its simplest forms it is a rearrangement of the furniture or a change of meals; in less simple forms it is the escape from **familiar** into unfamiliar companionship; in its rarest form, it is the enjoyment of works of art. As Whitehead says: "The fertilization of the soul is the reason for the necessity of art. A static value, however serious and important, becomes unendurable by its appalling monotony of endurance. The soul cries aloud for release into change. It suffers the agonies of claustrophobia. The transitions of humor, wit, irrelevance, play, sleep, and—above all—of art are necessary for it. Great art is the arrangement of the environment so as to provide for the soul vivid, but transient, values. Human beings require something that absorbs them for a time, something out of the routine which they can stare at. But you cannot subdivide life, except in the abstract analysis of thought. Accordingly, great art is more than a transient refreshment. It is something which adds to the permanent richness of the soul's self-attainment." [2] Works of art, in fact, are the most effectual expressions of the horizon of experience, which should be enjoyed in leisure.

The connection, however, between rearranging the furniture in a room and painting a picture is not usually understood, because a false tradition has severed the fine arts from the common life of ordinary folk. But the same impulse is satisfied in

---

[2] A. N. Whitehead's "Science and the Modern World," p. 251 (ed. 1927).

both cases, in the control of the environment or the discovery of new possibilities. This creativeness should find outlets in leisure, by the force of an "inner" life in each man. What particular outlet is best for each man, can be discovered only by him —not, indeed, in isolation, but certainly "for himself." Indeed it may be necessary to answer any one who asks what he ought to do with his leisure, in Nietzsche's phrase— "Here is my way; where is yours? . . . So I answered him who asked for *the* way: for *the* way existeth not." In the terms of a philosophy of life, leisure is the opportunity for each man to discover his own personality; and nobody else can do that for him; nor can any one else be "expert" enough to tell him the way. Such a philosophy, however, does not imply approval of a restless activity in "doing things"—playing games or reading books. Personality is not so completely hidden as to need continual probing. There was a man who "hid his talents in a napkin" and then shook the napkin by all four corners; and nothing came out! There may be no talent in your napkin; but if there is, its discovery is not dependent upon restless activity. Perhaps doing nothing would be best of all the uses of leisure.

The greatest skill is required for doing "nothing"; because it is easily confused with physical or mental sleep. Many a traveler among peoples whom the traveler regarded as barbarians, has expressed discomfort at the sight of men and women "doing nothing" apparently because, to the traveler's mind, they were "wasting time." The pernicious heresy of the nineteenth century that "time is money" led to a saving of time which was even worse than saving money; for saving time meant doing so much that nobody had any time to think about it. Certainly inertia or lack of energy is undesirable; and many "saints" have made the excuse that they were meditating a cover for their natural laziness. Perhaps much of the "spiritual life" that is thought to be Eastern, is merely medieval laziness; for there is no virtue in starving because the labor of producing food is distasteful. But undoubtedly the typical "business man" of the West suffers from a vice which is in the opposite extreme; it is the vice of restlessness. Such restlessness, of mind as well as of body, is disguised by the excuse that work is noble or that being energetic is being "alive." Between the extremes of laziness and business lies the true virtue of doing nothing.

Doing nothing is allowing freedom to the flow of one's perceptions and sensations and thoughts and emotions. It is awakening to the hundred facts and values to which we cannot afford to attend in the ordinary course of life. It is Aristotle's "contemplation"; and it may be "the dark night of the soul," according to St. John of the Cross. It is the passivity of the ideal scientist in observation and the activity of the ideal artist in designing what is to move the mass. The scientist is awake enough, although he "does nothing." The artist is "doing nothing" at the center of his personality, although his hands move.

This doing nothing is the one security against the danger that our "doing something" shall not be quite futile; for unless the life of a man is real to him in a sense quite distinct from that in which it is real to others, he has no refuge from externalism —not even in the hope for a better time to come after ours, which seems to support the most generous of men. The last illusion of noble minds is not ambition—which indeed affects only the simple-minded—but the belief that the present is merely a means toward a more desirable future. That belief is an inheritance, in the modern mythology of "progress," from the more ancient mythology of an "other world."

There is indeed an "other world"—indeed, as it was shown above, many of them. But they are not divided by the clock; one does not come after the other. If the metaphor were not equally misleading to any one who is ignorant of the facts, it would be possible to say that one world was within the other. In any case, present experience has intrinsic worth; its value is not altogether derived from its place in a sequence. Leisure, as indicated above, is well used to review the existing world and to "remold it nearer to the heart's desire": but leisure is also an opportunity for living in one's own right. It sounds noble to say that one lives for others; but in fact it is very bad for those others. Selfishness and self-realization are equally absurd as final purposes. At the point at which one passes into the most perfect form of doing nothing, there is no "purpose" at all —no conceived end—no "self" or what not—for the sake of which one is "doing nothing." One may reform the police-system or improve the drainage for the sake of others; one may eat a good dinner for self-realization; but one does not "live" *for* anything at all. One just lives. The perception of that fact and of its importance may very well come from doing nothing.

So hopelessly inadequate is language for any use outside the world of breakfast and dinner that the attempt to state such facts as these has an air, to some, of paradox and, to others, of platitude. Perhaps to yet another sort, it has no meaning at all; and if any one said that it had none, he could not be persuaded that he was wrong. Leisure in its finest form is not a suitable subject for an argument. To spend it in doing nothing may be the best any one can do; but to explain why that is so may perhaps be impossible.

APPENDIX

APPENDIX

The following letters, selected from a very large number, were written to me after the "Talks" upon which the chapters of this book are based. Those selected represent three different views: (a) the opposition to what is new, (b) relief at improvement, and (c) an implied desire in youth and maturity.

Yorkshire

Dear Sir,

Certainly our home life has changed! very much for the worse. You must know while you are speaking of the "more leisure," more entertainment "out of the house," and more "getting about" from one place to another, that it is all a most deplorable state of things. The young people *of all classes* are much less contented and happy than they were 25 or 30 years ago. We had a good class of domestic servant, from a good home where she had been well brought up and trained by a steady home-keeping mother. *Better educated* than now-a-days, and with much nicer tastes and ideas, and respect for themselves. We looked upon them as friends and appreciated what they did for us. The absence of proper domestic help is making the greatest change in the home. Accomplished, intelligent women are no longer companionable to their husbands, being worn out with having had to work all day at household duties for which they are not fitted and to do which they are ready to pay good servants. They are no longer a help to their children with for example, home lessons, accompanying violin practice on the piano, or the hundred and one things we did in my day, when our girls and boys were happy at home in a well ordered household with *rational* conversation and society. Can *any one* say that "this freedom," young girls having latch-keys and staying out late at night and coming home in cars with scarcely known acquaintances and having no doubt indulged too freely in cocktails is good? Everybody knows this is what is going on.

You will say—"You are one who has always lived in good homes and had good things around you, one who lives a tradition," and therefore I may be supposed to have no understanding or sympathy with those less favorably stationed, but that is not so. I submit that the working class is *not* so happy under the present conditions of more money, more leisure, and more ease in getting about. They are unsettled and cannot make themselves happy. Those village "Halls" used weekly for dances are a great source of evil, and you know as well as I do that young girls and lads leaving school simply set out to qualify for the dole. Wages are nearly treble for the same work, that they were 25 years ago and yet no domestic servant now has money to send home to her parents. No, she requires to be paid *weekly* very often and spends everything as it comes in. Foolish and unsuitable dress for her *own* use, and so poorly equipped for even *decency* that they have to be given clothing for their work in a house. Women of my age and experience are nothing less than disgruntled.

"A Scotswoman of 71"

APPENDIX

Gloucestershire, England

(Notes on the reactions of the population of an agricultural area to recent social changes and in reference to recent "Broadcast Talks.")

It is doubtful if the speaker quite knows the extent and number of the changes.

The son of a village shoemaker, I learnt his trade, then became (for 25 years) Sexton and parish Clerk, also for four generations my (woman) forebears were herbalists. One of my earliest recollections is the sight of women with bad legs and breasts, being treated. As a child, gathering herbs to make ointment, inspired me to get a knowledge of botany.

The writer of this had what was perhaps a unique opportunity, starting fifty years, ago, of personally knowing the whole population (1,800) in an area 5 by 4 miles. His work in the winter was killing pigs at the people's houses for home curing and consumption. These people included all the farmers, most of the laborers, the craftsmen such as masons, carpenters, blacksmiths, perhaps a dozen railway workers, as signalmen, porters and platelayers. Also six grocery stores where bacon was sold, much of it fed by themselves and nearly all of it fed locally.

Change I. This work has now ceased. There was a time when the absence of the cottager's pig meant extreme poverty, or a lack of thrift. With a meager wage and a family, to feed the pig involved a struggle, but even then, the bacon must not be eaten extravagantly or the very low cost would be no benefit. Now the laborer is better off and the fish cart, butcher's cart, grocer, baker, oilman, attend frequently on every mile of country by-road and the cottager lives like the townsman, "from hand to mouth." His diet has altered and bacon is largely replaced by sugar and tropical fruits.

Change II. May be put in few words. The word cart was used above without thought. The last "cart" vanished last year, they are all motors now.

Change III. Religion. The life of the average laborer used to be in two dimensions, his work and his home. There was no third. Perhaps about one third took an interest in religion. The laborer's social betters, as farmers tradesmen, etc., nearly all paid at least lip service to some form of religion. Now the attendance at the various places of worship is down to about one fifth of what it was, say forty-five years ago. At the beginning of the nineteenth century the only place of worship in the parish was the parish church, large enough to seat the whole population as it is now. Then the Methodists and Wesleyans started and in the ensuing seventy years built six more. When they had finished, the church woke up and built three. Looking back one might say, when the church began to build, the age of indifference had started to come and nothing could stop it.

Change IV. Population question. A few months ago, the vicar and a few local notables were gathered in the Village (National) School. It was pointed out to them that whereas the number of children on the books fifty years ago was over 200 the number now was 90. The Vicar and his friends seemed unable to believe or understand it. They thought there must be a catch in it. There are two other schools concerned and exact information would be difficult to get: so the following figures are estimates. In fifty years the population has fallen from 1,900 to 1,700. Of this fall 100 would be children of school age. Very little of this would be due to birth control, still less to the war. Birth control **has** now definitely set in and its effects will be increasingly felt in this village school.

One remark needs to be made here about birth control. It has been much stressed that instruction should be given to the poorest, for them to avoid having children which they can ill afford to rear. It may be and probably is true that the country worker and still more his wife are more intelligent than townsfolk. One enumerator at the last census was astonished at the clerking abilities of the laborer's wife. She seemed to be quite superior to her social betters at the farm; and *she has given up having children when they are not wanted.*

Just what this greatest and most amazing change will mean in the future, it is difficult to say. The writer of this has read "much argument about it and about," but never anything where the writer seemed to realize the vast importance of the subect. He may be a parson bemoaning the plenitude of "sin" or a soldier (Brass Hat) the scarcity of gun fodder or a slum-worker appalled at the things she has seen: but all seemed to be too much the victims of ignorance and emotion for their opinions to be worth anything.

Closely touching the above is:

Change V. The changing personnel amongst the farmers. Near the end of the last century much of the land was farmed by families that had been continuously in possession for two centuries or more. These have nearly all gone, not merely the names, but no blood relation remaining. One family has vanished like this after a stay of six centuries. Most of their successors are descended from "workers" and the tradition of work is still with them. They work hard and many hours. Education, religion, politics, culture of any kind, other than the soil, are little regarded. One thing may be said, they are not snobs, other than that their outlook is of the narrowest and most reactionary kind.

Compared with these men's wives many a laborer's wife is a lady of leisure and culture.

Change VI. Politics and social outlook. Starting at or near the end of the eighteenth century, the Wesleyans and Methodists captured perhaps half the farmers, and these were not tenant farmers. The tenant farmers were more fugitive. No great mansion dominated the land, and these yeomen, liberal in politics, represented the cultural level up to which the laborers looked. The yeomen are gone, religion is discredited, and in a cultural sense nobody looks *up* to anybody. The results so far are scant, perhaps there has not been time. The Liberals are gone, a few of the laborers have gone "Labor." The rest have gone Tory. The effect on some of the laborers of the better condition would seem to be a tendency to snobbishness. It may be that the mental reaction to the new conditions is mainly one of confusion. These people know nothing of "economics" and the much talked of increase of national wealth is not apparent on the country-side. The enjoyment of these new amenities is made to look illicit. "The country can't possibly afford it, bus rides! novels!! silk stockings!!!"

A significant feature is the appearance and total disappearance in little more than a century of the Wesleyan and Methodist farmer. It seems analogous to the case of the Quakers who came and went just previously.

Herne Bay, England

Dear Sir,

With reference to your talk to-night: "Has your Home changed?" The answer is: most decidedly, Yes.

APPENDIX

Going back to my boyhood days—50 years—the changes in the modern home are almost miraculous.

What strikes me most forcibly, and stands out to my mind in front of all the other modern, and up-to-date inventions, in the home are:

(1) Water; (2) firing; (3) lights; (4) sanitation.

(1) I can recall my father getting the necessary supply from the "spring" by means of buckets, with "yokes" over his shoulders. Later, obtaining the water from a well; and before I left home we obtained a supply by merely turning a tap.

(2) To get a fire in the morning, for the purpose of cooking the food, was at times a "nightmare," especially, when the wood was damp. Again I see my father, endeavouring to ignite the coal by endless "blowing" with the bellows. He lived to see the "breakfast," from the time of getting up, all ready in 10 to 15 minutes, by merely striking a match.

(3) My father hated the smell of paraffin, so perforce mother was obliged to use the "farthing dip" or rush light, varied by the ordinary tallow candle, the smell of which, when extinguished, was far worse than paraffin and most objectionable, and I, in my turn, object to the smell worse than anything I know to this day. Dad lived to use the gas. He prophesied "that Electricity was in its infancy, and no doubt we should get light from it, but it won't be in my time," he added.

(4) Sanitation. My first recollection was the old "earth closets" (abominations). Many years later, "cesspools," with our drinking water "well" about 10 yards distant therefrom.

Now, I ask, how can the present generation form any idea what their parents and grandparents had to contend with in the "services" referred to?

Another "time and labor" device is of untold value, that may be overlooked, because it is now so common and in general use, is: "Tiled hearths." When I was a boy, I was called upon to assist my sister in house-work and it was my job to black-lead the hearth, etc. It was the bane of my life. The time taken to get a polish was enormous. This was a daily routine. How I hated the job. The mess, too! Now, my wife or daughter, sometimes myself, with one flick of the duster and Hey presto, the hearth is done. Then, too, cleaning the brass and steel fenders, scraping the brick, adding oil, or paraffin, mixing to a paste, then rubbing off afterwards and polishing. The time! If these fenders are not now displaced altogether, they are oxidised and require no cleaning whatever.

Twelve years ago I invested in a dozen stainless knives. This investment proved the greatest of my life. There is nothing in the house so effective. Just think—after every meal, these said knives had to be cleaned by means of brick dust and a board (until we invested in a "knife cleaner").

The change of course is all for the best, but I will not admit we are happier or better off.

I must apologize for the length of this summary, and I must also ask you to take into consideration the difficulty I have had in putting this together, as my family are all "talking" and the wireless is in full swing.

Dunblane, Scotland

Dear Sir,

I have listened with keen interest to some of your radio talks on modern life and modern leisure. In the last one "The Youth of To-day" you asked for listeners' opinions on the subject and as I fall under the category with which you dealt, being a youth of twenty-five, I have decided to reply. If my few words fail to interest you I apologize for wasting your time.

In the first place when comparing relations between the sexes to-day with those of thirty years ago a distinct line must be drawn between the youth of the several fairly large towns and the innumerable country places. I have had a moderate experience of both country places and towns and am able therefore, I hope, to draw up a fair comparison.

I was not, of course, born thirty years ago and cannot speak with certainty but I feel sure that relations in the country between the youth of both sexes then and now are very similar. That is to say they have not yet acquired in the country that impersonal, platonic touch which is necessary to the development of a happy free "pally" relationship which is now manifest in any large town.

The fault lies, I think, not in the youth themselves but in the very nature of their environment. Things move slowly in the country place. There is not much to talk about and as people *must* talk (especially women) what is more interesting to gossip over than who so-and-so was seen talking to, who so-and-so danced with, with whom so-and-so went to the pictures.

There is no escape, and there is nothing so objectionable to modern youth as slanderous and suspicious observation. The certain knowledge that every innocent movement is being closely and furtively observed and maliciously misconstrued tends slowly to suffocate the healthy desire of modern youth to mix freely. In some places they can't do it. It is not done. In fact in places such as these when two people of different sex are seen together twice, heads begin to nod and tongues to wag (which may be quite harmless no doubt, but frightfully depressing when one has to live amongst it).

The town, on the other hand, gives modern youth a chance. Everything encourages a happy unfettered sociability between the young people. Everything is natural. Parents never come into the scheme at all or ever want to do so. Everybody is too busy living himself or herself to take anything but a passing interest in his or her friends "intentions" to so-and-so. Everybody lives (at least tries to, nowadays).

At least this is my experience. Young people can mix socially in all sorts of places, restaurants, dance halls, skating rinks, swimming baths, public parks, boating ponds, concert halls, the list is inexhaustible, and they all lend themselves to free social intercourse. That is the very essence of their being.

What a change to the stiff, narrow little meeting of the country church social union (sometimes the only public function) where every one present knows the history of every other from birth and where it were madness for any youthful person, who was foolish enough to go, to do other than look at his feet or, for a change, lift them in pious reverence to the roof.

The town spells "escape" to youth, natural freedom and equality. The country jogs along thirty years behind the times with its one redeeming feature "the golf course," without which Heaven help the "stranger."

FROM AN INTERESTED YOUTH IN THE COUNTRY

Blackpool

I might mention that after managing our own confectionery business for twenty-one years, I am kind of charring, half the week. I do not feel any loss of dignity or commoner through doing such common tasks. Yet how house-work and servanting are looked down on! I feel as much a "lady" as I did when in a bigger position. It is through feeling other things in the world of one's imagination, being interested in many discussions, religious happenings, etc.

Because I love to get away sometimes from everything and everybody, to go to where there is nothing, I am thought queer. Such an inner peace comes over me when in trouble I have gone where there is nothing. Would that doctors would prescribe such medicine!

I hear of many of my acquaintances never being idle. You defend those of us who like to be idle. What thoughts come into one's mind. One can't "think" really when one is doing something. But, as you say, people who can't be with their own thoughts must be amused—entertained. Children the same. What poor invalids they will make! I stick up for peaceful Sundays. To others, people who are hanging about look bored; but they are not: just letting the world slip into their minds, as you say. Peacefulness has not harmed country people—judging by their manners, looks—so often, great age. You are right about cultivating an "inner life." I used, in the midst of serving pies, groceries, etc., to very ordinary folk, to be preparing my Sunday-school lesson. Now, doing the most menial tasks of a house, I am saying over to myself some Francis Thompson or similar.

FROM A CHARWOMAN

INDEX

Adolescence, 52, 178 et seq.
Adult education, 137
Aëroplane, 55, 65
Amiel, 211
Art, 280
Asceticism, 108

Baden-Powell, 169
Beeching, 59
Bell, Clive, 203
Betting, 98 et seq.
Birth control, 151
Birth-rate, 157, 158
Bookmakers, 100
Boy Scouts, 165 et seq.

Calderon, G., 70
Castiglione, 232
Cavalcanti, G., 232
Chicago, 83, 84
Children, 45, 51-54, 130, 151, 158 et seq.
Chinese, 84, 185
Churches, 112-113, 188
Citizenship, 113
Class distinctions, 20-22, 63
Climbing, social, 214
Clothing, 19-21, 29, 30
Clubs, 277
Communists, 156, 264
Community Centers, 276, 277
Companies, 13
Conrad, 118, 119
Conventions, 115 et seq.
Creevy, 58
Crowds, 227, 228

Dante, 232
Democracy, 64, 72, 239
Diagram, 183

Education, 33, 38, 39, 82, 172, 173, 200
Eight-hour day, 264
Equality, 51, 64
Evening dress, 117
Excitement, 102 et seq.
Experimentalism, 36

Family, 159, 160, 171
Family income, 11, 160
Fear, 197
Flecker, 244
Food, 17 et seq.
France, 126
Furniture, 42

Gambling, 97, 98
Gasset, Ortega, 25
Gentleman, 132, 221
Germany, 141, 144, 172, 192
Gilbert, 229
Girl Guides, 165
Glasgow, 61
Great Britain, 60, 126, 141, 176, 184

Hall, Stanley, 184
Hiking, 104, 187
Hobson, J. A., 214
Holidays, 206
Home, 50, 91
Houses, 47, 48

INDEX

Housing area, 47
Husband, 49

Ideals, 201
I.L.O., 263, 264
Individuality, 23
Inner life, 251, 252
Intimacy, 52, 53, 67
Italy, 156, 193, 264

Lady, 221
Leisured class, 137, 201
London, 61

Maeterlinck, 43
Manners, 63, 115, 123, 129, 189
Marriage, 148 et seq.
Mass, 22, 24
Mencken, 142
Mill, John S., 51
Montague, 213
Morality, 196 et seq.
Morgan, C., 252
Motor-cars, 55
Movements, 137
Movies, 75 et seq., 161

National Playing Fields Association, 121, 164
Nature, 105, 187
News, 113

"Opera Nazionale Dopolavoro," 265
Originality, 23

Parents, 51 et seq.
Play, 155
Public services, 12
Putnam, E. J., 231

Quiet, 104, 249

Radio, 75 et seq.
Relativity, 65
Restaurants, 18
Rest-days, 259

Roads, 57
Rural areas, 62
Rush, 69
Russia, 165, 193, 264

Sabbath, 260
Saint, 223
Saints' days, 260 et seq.
Saving, 261
Schools, 51
Sex appeal, 89, 184, 199
Sextus Empiricus, 256
Sexual ethics, 146, 150, 197
Similarity, 77, 174
Speed, 65
Standardization, 23, 234
Students, 194
Suffrage Movement, 141 et seq.
Sunday, 112, 121, 259
Superficiality, 66
Superior persons, 122

Tea-shops, 18, 31
Tocqueville, 236
Town life, 127
Troelsch, 221

United States, 158, 182, 185, 216

Veblen, 212

Wages, 10
War, 158, 192
Weber, Max, 221
Welfare, 264
Wells, H. G., 42, 214, 215
Whitehead, 280
Wife, 49
Women, 31, 50, 140
Women Citizens, 143
Women's Institutes, 143
Women's work, 147

Youth hostels, 106
Youth Movement, 192